Books
by Gore Vidal

An Evening
with Richard Nixon

An Evening
with Richard Nixon
by Gore Vidal

and Richard Nixon, Gloria Steinem,
George Washington, John F. Kennedy,
Thelma (Pat) Nixon, Nikita Khrushchev,
Dwight D. Eisenhower, Spiro T. Agnew,
Hannah Milhous Nixon,
Lyndon B. Johnson, Lt. William Calley, Jr.,
Hubert H. Humphrey, Martha Mitchell,
Jerry Voorhis, Helen Gahagan Douglas,
Harry S Truman, Adlai E. Stevenson,
Murray Chotiner, Patricia (Tricia) Nixon,
Howard K. Smith, etc.

Random House 🏠 New York

ISBN: 0-394-48007-4
Library of Congress Catalog Card Number: 72-37424

Manufactured in the United States of America
by Haddon Craftsmen, Scranton, Pa.
9 8 7 6 5 4 3 2

For J. Edgar Hoover and Clyde Tolson
With Appreciation

Note

In 1960 the Democratic National Committee sent out a good deal of advice to the party's congressional candidates. I remember nothing they sent me except the warning: Don't mention Nixon's slush fund or the Little Dog Checkers speech or anything else to do with Nixon's past, because the voters have forgotten and if you try to remind them they'll become seriously annoyed and think they are back in school trying to recall who Alexander Hamilton was. This made a great impression on me. Although only eight years had passed since Nixon had celebrated his love for what I had always thought was quite a decent spaniel (despite the kind of rumor you are apt to hear about any dog in public life), the subject was taboo. Nixon— we—had no past.

Over the years I have spoken about politics to quite a few audiences and I'm continually struck by their collective ignorance—or perhaps lack of memory is a more tactful way of putting it. They don't know who did what last week much less ten years ago, and they don't want to be told. This of course, plays into the hands of the politician. He can reinvent himself every morning. Edward Kennedy's Presidential campaign will doubtless feature him as The Hero of Chappaquiddick—the man who swam twenty miles with a wounded secretary under one arm. CHAPPAQUIDDICK AND HUMPHREY, TOO!

The idea for an evening with Richard Nixon came to me after much brooding on the national amnesia. I decided that I would put into a single two-hour "entertainment" the thirty-seventh President's career, using his own words—and those of others. At the end of this narrative it won't be possible for anyone to say, Oh, I'm sure he never said that about China, or Truman, or price controls—or compared his invasion of Cambodia with the Soviet's invasion of Czechoslovakia. Here it all is from the beginning to a few months ago.

The statements actually made by Nixon and the other players are done in this sort of type. The dialogue which I have invented is in this sort of type. At the back of the book I have listed all the Nixon quotations and their sources. I wanted to do this for Kennedy, Eisenhower, Agnew, etcetera, but the cost was prohibitive; their quotations, however, are all a matter of public record except for Goldwater's remark to me about Nixon's campaign of 1960 when, said the Senator thoughtfully, "Nixon just went sashayin' around the country like shit through a canebrake." I don't think Barry—one of the few people in this narrative who comes through as an honest man —will mind my quoting him.

Particular thanks are due the gallant Helen Hopps who has spent many months researching Nixon for me.

G.V.

Phase One

The curtain is up. A black backdrop onto which will be cast suitable pictures, still and moving, as well as names, statistics, etc. Center stage, on a platform: a red, white and blue cherry tree (with stars for leaves) has been hacked down. An ax lies beside it. Whenever a table, a desk, a chair is needed, it will just appear—and disappear—as desired. A figure in eighteenth-century costume hurries on stage.

WASHINGTON *(Diffidently)* Good evening, ladies and gentlemen. My name is George Washington. Your first President. *General* George Washington? You know . . . "First in war, first in peace." *(He looks about somewhat anxiously, as though not quite certain he is getting through)*

VOICE OVER *(Stentorian, godlike)* Who cut down that cherry tree?

WASHINGTON Later, Father. *(To the audience)* I cannot tell a lie. Remember? *(Removes a thick scroll from his jacket)* Tonight it gives me . . . uh, great pleasure to introduce Richard Milhous Nixon, one of the Presidents who came after me . . . in fact, who is still coming after me, as he is currently your President . . . *(We hear Nixon's voice over, saying whatever it is that he has been saying the day of this particular performance)*

NIXON'S VOICE OVER By devaluating the dollar— something this administration will never do—there will be greater prosperity for all Americans both here and abroad . . . *(Something along that order . . . Washington makes a gesture. The voice stops.)*

WASHINGTON That's enough, thank you. Now for a quick survey of the thirty-seventh President's early days, the great moments of his career— *(Glances at scroll)*—or in this case, the great crises . . . *(Eisenhower enters, holding a golf club)* There you are, General . . . uh, now, now, don't tell me . . . I know . . . I know . . .

EISENHOWER Eisenhower. And you're . . . You're . . . uh . . . Hamilton?

WASHINGTON Washington.

EISENHOWER Should've known . . . sorry . . . Wasn't briefed on that one . . . Not an expert in that area . . . but I do know the face . . .

WASHINGTON The wig?

EISENHOWER No. The dollar bill.

WASHINGTON Tonight we're doing a show for the living . . .

EISENHOWER Personally, I don't like shows. Television . . . now that's more my kinda thing . . . *Gunsmoke* . . . *Wyatt Earp* . . .

WASHINGTON Tonight we're doing Nixon.

EISENHOWER Doing *what* to Nixon?

WASHINGTON The works.

EISENHOWER *(Alarm)* He's not dead, is he?

WASHINGTON No. No.

EISENHOWER Whew! Thought we'd have him here. Biggest damn bore. Politics, politics . . . all he ever thinks of. *(Looks about)* What happened to the Ninth Hole?

WASHINGTON The what?

EISENHOWER Just a minute ago this was the Ninth Hole. *(Kennedy enters. Looking fit)*

EISENHOWER Well, look who's here, that smartass kid.

KENNEDY *(Crisply)* General Eisenhower . . .

EISENHOWER *(Curt nod)* Kennedy. This is General . . .

KENNEDY *(Promptly)* George Washington. Born 1732, died 1799. *(Shakes Washington's hand)* Always been a dream of mine, meeting you, sir.

WASHINGTON Thank you. *(Aside to Eisenhower)* Who's he?

EISENHOWER Kennedy. President after me.

WASHINGTON Looks too young.

EISENHOWER You can say that again. Worst goddam mistake I ever made was . . .

KENNEDY I heard there was going to be a Dick Nixon show tonight and you'd be needing me.

WASHINGTON Yes. That's if you were in any way involved with the President. I'm afraid I haven't read the script yet, but it says here that we'll be doing Mr. Nixon in *depth* . . .

KENNEDY *(Dryly)* You won't drown . . .

WASHINGTON I'm what they call the emcee. *(Looks about somewhat blankly; then a light cue)* Oh! Well, now

(5)

we're ready to start The Nixon Story. From the top . . .

KENNEDY   I don't know if I can take that "simple Quaker boy from Whittier" number . . .

EISENHOWER   Which happens to be stolen from my own "simple farm boy from Abilene . . ."

KENNEDY *(To Washington)*   I must warn you, General, Mr. Nixon is a very boring man . . .

EISENHOWER   He stole that from me, too . . .

KENNEDY   No. That was all his own. Why don't we do Lyndon instead?

WASHINGTON   Because a directive has come down asking us to explain Mr. Nixon in *his own words* to the people still living. And orders are orders. Particularly for us, as military men. *(To Kennedy)* You were a military man . . .?

EISENHOWER *(Chuckles)*   I'll say! *(To Kennedy)* Tell General Washington about how you managed to get that dinky little boat of yours in front of that big Japanese boat and how it ran over you.

KENNEDY   So how far can *you* swim, Ike? *(The lights change. The Nixon family house appears on screen)*

WASHINGTON *(Reads)*   Here we are in Yorba Linda, California . . . Linda Yorba? *(Looks up)* Yorba Linda is what it says here . . . *(Hannah and a nurse enter and stand center stage. Hannah does not look pregnant, simply stolid. The three dead Presidents retreat to stage right. Washington reads)* It is January 9, 1913. Nine thirty-five P.M. Hannah, the saintly Quaker, is delivered of an eleven-pound boy, Richard Milhous Nixon. *(Nixon appears from behind Hannah, dressed as he is always dressed: in a blue suit, all set to run for President. Characteristically, his eyes dart this way and that)*

KENNEDY He looks as if he expects somebody to throw something.

WASHINGTON *(Reads)* It is his first crisis.

EISENHOWER *(Irritably)* You know, that title he used? *Six Crises?* He stole it from Beetle Smith's book about me, *Six Decisions* . . .

WASHINGTON *(Hushes him)* Please, General. This is the story of our *living* President. *(Hannah Nixon recites in a solemn monotone)*

HANNAH It is difficult at times to understand the ways of our Lord, but we know that there is a plan and the best happens for each individual.

WASHINGTON Henrietta Shockney was the nurse who assisted at the birth . . . *(Henrietta Shockney takes a dust rag and whisks it about Nixon's shoulders)*

HENRIETTA He was an unusually big baby, with a crop of black hair and a powerful, ringing voice. *(Henrietta starts offstage)* I believe he has retained both the hair and his voice. *(At the edge of the stage she stops)* All babies are more or less alike, and when one of them becomes famous we can ponder on the ways of fate. *(Exit Henrietta)*

HANNAH My mother was especially attached to Richard . . . While he was still in his teens she instilled in him his appreciation of and respect for our national heritage.

KENNEDY Oh . . . shit! Really, a little bit of this goes a long way . . .

EISENHOWER You should've seen the profile they did of you . . . how your grandfather Honey Fitz used to sing "Sweet Adeline" in the bars of Boston, that's when he wasn't in jail for fraud.

(7)

KENNEDY   I'd rather be in jail in Boston for fraud than in Whittier, California, at any time.

WASHINGTON   Gentlemen, this is for the living!

EISENHOWER   Wouldn't be in their shoes . . . next war . . . pow . . .!

WASHINGTON *(To the audience)*   I should remind you at this point that everything these people say *(Points to Nixon and Hannah)* they actually said. These are their actual words. Nothing is invented.

KENNEDY   Except us.

EISENHOWER   Speak for yourself. *I* don't feel invented. Never did.

WASHINGTON *(Reads the question to Hannah)*   Mrs. Nixon, do you believe there is such a thing as a *new* Nixon? *(During Hannah's following speech we see Nixon gravely miming the part of a serious person)*

HANNAH   No. He has always been exactly the same. I never knew a person to change so little. From the time he was first able to understand the world around him until now, he has reacted the same way to the same situations . . . He was very mature when he was five or six years old. He always carried such a weight. That's an expression we Quakers use for a person who doesn't take his responsibilities lightly.

WASHINGTON   Mr. Nixon, would you give us *your* impression of your childhood?

NIXON *(Formally)*   Thank you, General Washington, General Eisenhower, President Kennedy. *(To the audience)* Folks.   It is true that we had hardships but I should like to emphasize that we didn't consider them particularly hard. This was due, primarily, to the even temperament of

(8)

my mother. But there is no question that virtually everything any of us boys were to have, whether it was an education, a new suit, or the like, we had to work very hard for it.

EISENHOWER That's my boy.

NIXON I'll try to be worthy of your trust, General.

WASHINGTON That line is invented.

NIXON *(To audience)* We were poor but we didn't know it.

EISENHOWER Dammit, that's from *my* book!

KENNEDY *(Maliciously)* Same writer maybe?

EISENHOWER It wasn't Sorenson, let me tell you . . .

NIXON We not only learned the value of a dollar but also the importance of work, and at the same time we developed a high competitive spirit.

HANNAH I had hoped he would be a musician or a preacher. *(Nixon wanders up and down nervously. A train whistle sounds)*

NIXON That train whistle was the sweetest music I ever heard.

WASHINGTON *(Stares at his notes)* Your father was called Frank . . . *(Frank Nixon enters. Glowers. Wields a leather belt. Nixon edges away nervously)*

NIXON I learned early that the only way to deal with him was to abide by the rules he laid down. Otherwise, I would probably have felt the touch of the ruler or the strap as my brothers did. *(During this, Nixon has crossed to a table on which sits a bowl filled with potatoes; he begins expertly to mash them. Frank goes offstage)*

HANNAH He was the best potato masher one could wish for. Even when I visited Richard and Pat in Washington or when they visited me he would take over the potato mashing. My feeling is that he actually enjoyed it. *(But Nixon is not enjoying it. He is just grimly doing his duty. Harriet Palmer Hudspeth appears)*

WASHINGTON He used to date Harriet Palmer Hudspeth.

KENNEDY I don't believe it.

HARRIET Oh, he used to dislike us girls so! He would make horrible faces at us. As a debater his main theme in grammar school and in the first years of high school was why he hated girls. One thing was strange, though. He said he didn't like us, but he didn't seem to mind arguing with us. *(With a saucy toss of her head, she is gone. Nixon at the potato bowl gives her a look calculated to kill)*

EISENHOWER Never said he was a regular fellow but even so . . .

KENNEDY I remember once when we were in the Senate . . .

WASHINGTON *(Valley Forge)* Will you two shut up? That's an order. *(The two obey. Nixon is at his potatoes, aware of everything that is being said. Hannah stares glassily ahead)*

HANNAH It was during the Teapot Dome scandal. *(A montage of oil derricks on the back screen: oil money is a constant theme in Nixon's financial life)* Day after day the papers headlined stories of corruption in the handling of the government oil reserves. One day Richard was lying in front of the fireplace with newspapers spread all over the floor. Suddenly he said . . .

NIXON *(Childish treble)* Mother, I would like to become a lawyer—an honest lawyer who can't be bought by crooks.

WASHINGTON That's very . . . moving.

KENNEDY Yes. I am moved, too. Nixon has served the oil interests almost as loyally as Lyndon. The oil people paid for Nixon's slush fund, they paid for his first campaign, they . . .

EISENHOWER Just because certain businessmen are by nature conservationists . . .

KENNEDY I think you mean conservative.

EISENHOWER That's what I said—doesn't mean they aren't good Americans . . .

KENNEDY Come to think of it, the oil men paid for the livestock at your farm in Gettysburg.

EISENHOWER *(Boiling)* Just the way your father paid for your election . . .

WASHINGTON Gentlemen, Mr. Nixon is at a great disadvantage. He is programmed to say only what he has actually said over the years which means he can't answer you even though everything you say he hears —actually, he thinks he's having a nightmare in the guest bedroom of Bebe Rebozo.

KENNEDY Tell him to stop with those damned potatoes.

WASHINGTON *(To Nixon)* That's enough, I think . . . *(Nixon gratefully puts down the potato masher. To Nixon)* Early jobs? *(Nixon acts out early jobs, against appropriate background pictures)*

NIXON Picking string beans, washing vegetables, polishing apples, janitor at a public swimming pool, handyman and sweeper in a packing house, barker for the Wheel of Chance at the Slippery Gulch Rodeo in Prescott, Arizona . . .

(11)

WASHINGTON *(Reads)* This was the legal front for a concession where, in the back room, there was poker and dice . . .

NIXON *(Shamefaced)* Yes, General.

HANNAH As far back as high school, Richard was always running for some office, but I suppose his first real test was in 1933. He was a junior at Whittier College and he was trying to get elected president of the Student Body. *(Nixon starts to wander about the stage awkwardly, shaking imaginary hands)* Then, as now, he was a realist blessed with a facility for reconciling ideas and facts.

WASHINGTON He won the election. He also played football . . . *(Nixon begins to scamper about, throwing imaginary balls, trying to catch—and missing—them. Coach enters. Points sternly at a bench. Nixon falls onto it)*

COACH *(To the audience)* He was wonderful for morale because he'd sit there and cheer the rest of the guys. *(Nixon cheers invisible team)* And tell them how well they played. To sit on a bench for four years isn't easy . . . *(Coach departs)*

WASHINGTON *(Reads)* Then . . . on to Duke University law school. *(Nixon rises, joined by a fellow student, wearing cap and gown)*

NIXON I'm scared. I counted twenty-four Phi Beta Kappa keys in my class. I don't believe I can stay up top in that group.

STUDENT Listen, Nixon, you needn't worry. You don't mind hard work. You've got an iron butt, and that's the secret of becoming a lawyer. *(Nixon looks pleased. Pats his iron butt. The student addresses the audience)* Dick appeared from the very beginning as a true liberal. Dick never felt an

(12)

individual could transfer his responsibilities to the government and at the same time keep his freedom.

KENNEDY   *That's* liberalism?

EISENHOWER   You bet it is.

NIXON   I won my share of scholarships and of speaking and debating prizes, not because I was smarter but because I worked longer and harder than some of my gifted colleagues.

STUDENT   We called him Gloomy Gus.

NIXON *(Plaintively)*   Call me Nix.

STUDENT   Once Gus crawled in through the transom of the Dean's office to look at his grades. *(Student goes off. Coach enters)*

WASHINGTON   He still wanted to play football. *(Nixon charges about, uncoordinatedly)*

COACH   Many men at Duke no heavier than Dick have been first-rate players. What he lacks is the capacity of the natural athlete to react instinctively. His reactions are governed by his conscious thought processes . . . *(The student reappears, tackles Nixon, who falls with a crash. Gamely, Nixon gets up)* He had two left feet. *(Student tackles Nixon. He falls)* We used Dick for purposes of dummy tackling . . . *(Nixon gets up; is tackled again)*

KENNEDY *(Intones)*   On the playing fields of Whittier and Duke the iron entered his soul.

EISENHOWER   I had a trick knee . . . Kept me on the bench quite a lot.

KENNEDY   I had a trick back . . . Got it playing touch football . . .

WASHINGTON *(Politely)*   I am sure football is excellent training for a Chief Executive. *(Nixon has finally got away*

(13)

from the tackler. Straightens his suit, tie, hair. Washington consults the scroll)

WASHINGTON *(Reads)* He was generally quiet, peace-loving . . . according to his brother, Don . . . *(Some family-album photographs of the youthful Nixon boys)*

DON'S VOICE OVER When we had fights with neighbor boys, he would step in and talk us out of it.

NIXON *(Suddenly)* Negotiation not confrontation.

DON'S VOICE OVER He did not explode himself. He saved things up, though. Once I did something that finally got him angry, and he didn't just criticize me for that. He went back two years telling me all the things I had done wrong.

EISENHOWER Glad I treated him so well . . . always . . . Fact, I called him . . . uh, Dick. He called me . . . General. *(Nixon overhears this; scowls)*

NIXON *(To the audience)* General Eisenhower never asked me to see the upstairs at the White House where he lived. It was years before he asked me inside the house at Gettysburg . . .

EISENHOWER *(Coldly)* Is he talking about me . . .?

KENNEDY Yes! And that reminds me, when your wife showed Jackie through the White House—right after the baby—she never asked her to sit down . . .

EISENHOWER *(Tightly)* Why should she? You and your goddam missile gap when you knew we were ahead of the Commies three to one . . .

KENNEDY We all make mistakes, General.

NIXON *(Suddenly)* Eisenhower was a far more complex and devious man than most people realized . . .

EISENHOWER *(Grins suddenly)* I went out of office as popular as when I went in. That doesn't just happen.

NIXON *(Finishes)* . . . in the best sense of those words.

KENNEDY Doesn't he remind you of Uriah Heep?

EISENHOWER Doesn't remind me of a damn thing. *(Washington motions for them to be quiet)*

WASHINGTON Now the career is under way. Nixon applies for a job with the law firm Sullivan and Cromwell in New York. *(A blast of trumpets as the Wall Street tower containing Sullivan and Cromwell is shown. Nixon is standing at attention before imaginary employers, hearing bad news)* He was turned down. *(Nixon looks at the audience)*

NIXON If they had given me a job, I'm sure I would have been there today. I'd've been a corporation lawyer instead of President.

KENNEDY Wall Street's gain was the country's loss.

EISENHOWER Funny I can't imagine Dick being President. *(To Kennedy)* Or you for that matter.

KENNEDY What a coincidence.

WASHINGTON Please, gentlemen. *(Looks at the scroll)* In those days he was a liberal, it says here, but not a flaming liberal. And he applied for a job with his idol, J. Edgar Hoover at the FBI. *(Screen fills with a portrait of Hoover, circa 1937)*

EISENHOWER I've met that fellow somewhere . . . one of those bureaucrats, isn't he?

KENNEDY Sorry to say I kept him on. I had to. All those secret files . . . *(Nixon stands now in a state of exaltation, hands over his head, worshiping the icon of Hoover)*

WASHINGTON Nixon didn't get that job either. *(The picture fades. So does Nixon: arms are lowered . . . dejection. A desk and two chairs appear)* Nixon finally got a job with a law firm in Whittier where, according to his secretary, Evelyn Dorn . . .

EVELYN DORN'S VOICE OVER   His law experience was mainly probating and oil-leasing contracts. *(Nixon suddenly starts squeezing oranges on his desk)*

WASHINGTON   Nixon decided to become a capitalist with frozen orange juice. He called it Citra-Frost. For a year and a half he squeezed many of the oranges himself.

EVELYN DORN'S VOICE OVER   It was a great idea, as other attempts later proved, but we couldn't find the right container. The failure of Citra-Frost was a great disappointment to him.

KENNEDY *(To Washington)*   What about the sex-life, General?

WASHINGTON   We're coming to that. *(Nixon has seated himself at a desk. A splendid girl sits opposite him—he is distracted. Her lips never stop moving—nor the rest of her)*

NIXON'S VOICE OVER   When I just started law practice, I had a divorce case to handle, and this good-looking girl, beautiful really, began talking to me about her intimate marriage problems. I was so embarrassed I turned fifteen colors of the rainbow!

KENNEDY *(Disgust)*   Jesus!

WASHINGTON   According to his secretary he worked all the time, sending out for pineapple malts and hamburgers.

KENNEDY   Mashed potatoes, string beans, pineapple malts . . . Food keeps cropping up, doesn't it?

EISENHOWER   Me, I always did the cooking while Mamie did the . . . uh, washing up . . .

(16)

NIXON *(Solemnly)* The worst thing in the world is to eat heavy food when you have a lot of work to do.

WASHINGTON He met Pat in the winter of 1938. At the rehearsals of a play called *The Dark Tower. (Pat enters, holding a script; Nixon has picked up a script)*

NIXON *(To the audience)* A friend told me about the beautiful new teacher who was trying out for a part at the little theater. It was suggested that I go down and take a look . . . so I did and I liked what I saw.

WASHINGTON On their first date . . .

NIXON I'm going to marry you.

PAT I don't want to settle down yet.

NIXON Oh. *(That takes care of that. They part. Each goes to an opposite end of the stage)*

WASHINGTON According to Albert Upton, Nixon's drama coach, he was a good actor.

UPTON'S VOICE OVER I taught him how to cry in a play by John Drinkwater called *Bird in Hand.* It was beautifully done, those tears.

WASHINGTON Two years later Pat and Dick were married. *(Dick and Pat reunited, primly, center stage)*

KENNEDY Very touching story.

WASHINGTON Six months later . . . Pearl Harbor . . . *(Explosion. Shots of American fleet sinking)*

ROOSEVELT'S VOICE OVER . . . a day which will live in infamy, the United States of America was suddenly and deliberately attacked by the naval and air forces of the Empire of Japan.

EISENHOWER Marshall was out riding that morning. Poor intelligence work.

WASHINGTON Our hero . . .

KENNEDY Our *what?*

(17)

WASHINGTON *(Testily)* I'm reading the script. *(Reads)* Our hero went to Washington to offer his services to the government.

KENNEDY Why didn't he enlist?

WASHINGTON He joined the Office of Price Administration. He ceased to be a liberal.

EISENHOWER That's my boy.

NIXON *(Gravely)* At OPA, I saw that there were people who weren't interested in carrying out the regulations, but who had a passion for *getting* business and used the authority they had to that end. They were the remnants of the old die-hard New Deal.

KENNEDY Sounds like Dad.

NIXON *(To Kennedy)* A great American. *(To the audience)* I insisted on taking the lowest possible salary because the boys who were then being trained to hit the beaches were paid a lot less.

EISENHOWER *(Slow response)* Come to think of it, why didn't you enlist?

NIXON As a Quaker I could claim exemption. But I applied for a Naval commission and in September '42 I became a Lieutenant JG. *(Nixon puts on a naval hat)* I was sent to the Pacific. I was there when the bombs were falling.

WASHINGTON *(Reads)* He saw no enemy action.

NIXON I said I was there when the bombs were falling.

WASHINGTON That was at Bougainville. You were setting up cargo bases behind the lines. You were never in combat.

NIXON *(Fiercely)* Are you trying to say that I wasn't there when the bombs were falling?

WASHINGTON Technically, I suppose you were, but . . .

NIXON OK. So stop bugging me. *(Pulls himself together)* General Washington . . . *(To the audience)* . . . a great American whose loyalty no one can suspect . . .

WASHINGTON The last few lines of dialogue are invented. *(Reads)* Most of our hero's time was taken playing poker . . .

OFFICER'S VOICE OVER Nixon never lost, but he was never a big winner. He always played it close to the belt.

NIXON I never knew what poker was until I joined the Navy. *(Nixon shuffles cards like a sharp)*

OFFICER'S VOICE OVER On Green Island, he opened Nixon's Snack Shack where he traded everything from captured Japanese rifles to introductions to the Army nurses who arrived to take care of the casualties . . .

KENNEDY That's better.

EISENHOWER Free enterprise.

NIXON *(Quickly)* Nonprofit. *(To the audience)* Politics never occurred to me during this time.

KENNEDY I bet.

EISENHOWER *(To Kennedy)* Your dad was running you even then, eh?

KENNEDY So when did you start running?

EISENHOWER I didn't have to run. I was more like . . . uh, General Washington here . . .

KENNEDY That's not true. *(To the audience)* Eisenhower wanted to run as early as 1948 but General Patton's widow scared him off. You see, she had these letters and . . . *(Eisenhower looks ready for a stroke. Washington motions for silence. The screen is filled with cheering crowds—V-E Day in Times Square)*

(19)

WASHINGTON *(Through him)* The war ended. Nixon and Pat are in Washington. Wondering what to do. *(Nixon—still wearing the Navy hat—and Pat stand side by side, wondering what to do)* Back in California, a number of businessmen are holding a meeting in order to decide upon a Republican candidate for Congress to run against the liberal Democrat Jerry Voorhis. They have already put an ad in the paper, asking for volunteers.
KENNEDY This part is wild.
WASHINGTON One of the businessmen remembered Nixon. *(A telephone rings. Nixon answers it)*
VOICE FROM TELEPHONE Dick . . . are you a Republican?
NIXON *(Cautiously)* I guess so. I voted for Dewey.
VOICE FROM TELEPHONE How would you like to be Republican candidate from the twelfth district against . . . *(Nixon flies across the stage to address a group of businessmen; still wears naval cap)*
WASHINGTON He flew to California. He was selected at a meeting where he laid it on the line about the two schools of thought in America.
NIXON *(Firmly)* One, advocated by the New Deal, is government control regulating our lives. The other calls for individual freedom and all that initiative can produce. I hold with the latter viewpoint as do, I believe, the returning veterans—and I have talked to many of them in the foxholes . . . *(Nixon gives Washington a beady look. With a gesture Washington ends the scene)*
WASHINGTON The campaign began. A Los Angeles lawyer named Murray Chotiner—
NIXON Shott-ner . . .
WASHINGTON —took charge of his campaign. Mr. Chotiner was a new breed of political tactician . . .

CHOTINER'S VOICE OVER *(Like God)* Begin one full year ahead of election . . . because if you do not deflate the opposition candidate before your own candidate gets started, the odds are that you are going to be doomed to defeat.

KENNEDY *(To the voice)* What is the difference between legitimate attack and smear? *(To Eisenhower)* As if *we* don't know.

EISENHOWER Speak for yourself, bub. I never dealt in personalities.

CHOTINER'S VOICE OVER *(Like God)* It is not a smear, if you please, if you point out the record of your opponent . . . Of course it is always a smear, naturally, when it is directed to our own candidate. *(During this, Nixon has been jogging about the stage . . . getting ready for the big game. Pat enters, pushing ten seated dummies on a trolley. They are faceless; above them a sign says: "The American People." One face is black. They are set upstage center. Campaign workers appear. A long table with telephones. Two pedestals are rolled out, one to the left, one to the right of "The American People." Nixon starts shaking hands with everyone. Very grim)*

NIXON'S VOICE OVER We will put on a fighting, rocking, socking campaign!

WASHINGTON *(Reads)* Had Enough, Vote Republican! It was 1946. People were tired of Harry Truman. People were afraid of . . . *(Whisper)* Communism.

VOICE OVER Nixon is a clean, forthright young American who fought in defense of his country in the stinking mud and jungles of the Solomons . . . *(Nixon tenses at this; glances furtively at Washington to see if he will give the game away. Washington is studying the script. Nixon continues campaigning)* . . . while Congressman Voorhis stayed safely

(21)

behind the front in Washington. *(A young male voter looks at Nixon scornfully, walks away without shaking his hand)* Get out of that uniform, schmuck! GI's hate officers . . . *(Nixon throws away the cap. The young man then shakes his hand)*

WASHINGTON   In those days the Political Action Committee—or PAC—of the CIO labor union was thought to be Communist-controlled. Our hero decided that Congressman Voorhis ought to be connected with the PAC.

VOICE OVER   A vote for Nixon is a vote against socialization of free American institutions; against the PAC, its Communist principles and its gigantic slush fund. The present congressman from this district has consistently supported the socialization of free American institutions. *(Voorhis enters with an aide. Voorhis—like Helen Gahagan Douglas, Adlai Stevenson, Hubert Humphrey, etc.—will wear a mask (in his own image, needless to say): this means the same actor can play the parts of Nixon's various political opponents. Eisenhower and Kennedy also wear masks when they participate in Nixon's career. In limbo, they are like Washington, maskless. Nixon never wears a mask)*

VOORHIS   But the PAC are *not* supporting me. I am not a Communist. I have always been an anti-Communist. It is a matter of record published in newspapers throughout the state that the CIO Political Action Committee does *not* endorse my reelection.

AIDE   *(To Voorhis)* Debate the little bastard . . . Tell him off . . . *(Voorhis nods. Takes a position stage right on pedestal. Nixon gets on the pedestal stage left, paper in hand. A pause. At the table each campaign worker has a telephone, receiver to ear. In unison they whisper)*

(22)

CAMPAIGN WORKERS   This is a friend of yours. I just want you to know that Jerry Voorhis is a Communist. *(All hang up together. "The American People," who have been closer to Voorhis than to Nixon, roll slightly toward Nixon)*

NIXON   You were in favor of gas rationing . . .

VOORHIS   In wartime . . .

NIXON   Grain rationing . . .

VOORHIS   The war . . .

NIXON   Meat rationing. There are those walking in high official places who would destroy our constitutional principles . . .

VOORHIS   Now, look here . . .

NIXON   There are the people who front for un-American elements, wittingly or otherwise, by advocating increasing Federal controls over the lives of the people. Today the American people are faced with a choice between two philosophies of government: one of them supported by the radical PAC and its adherents . . .

VOORHIS   Of which I am not one.

NIXON *(Through him)*   . . . would deprive the people of liberty through regimentation. The other would return the government to the people . . .

VOORHIS   Let's get back to the PAC . . .

NIXON   By all means. *(Holds up a paper triumphantly)* Here is proof that they are endorsing you.

VOORHIS   They are not . . .

NIXON *(To "The American People")*   At a meeting in Los Angeles the local PAC recommends that the national PAC endorse Congressman Voorhis . . .

VOORHIS   But the recommendations were ignored, they did not endorse me and . . .

(23)

NIXON *(Through him)* Here is the proof! You can't argue with facts. *("The American People" lurch toward Nixon, who raises his arms in a victory salute. Pat looks at him, beaming proudly. Voorhis vanishes. For the first time in this psychopolitico drama Nixon smiles. The smile is hesitant, mechanical . . . Finally full; teeth bared: Victory)*

WASHINGTON Nixon won. Of course the Political Action Committee had never endorsed Voorhis but Nixon managed to confuse the issue. Referring to this campaign ten years later, Nixon said . . .

NIXON *(To the audience)* Communism was *not* the issue in the '46 campaign. Few people knew about Communism then, and even fewer cared.

KENNEDY Despicable.

EISENHOWER *(To Kennedy)* Missile gap.

WASHINGTON He's on his way to Washington now. To begin his career as a . . . well, a . . . uh, professional politician. *(Nixon and Pat are meeting a new set of people. An interviewer comes up to Nixon)*

INTERVIEWER Do you have any bill you plan to introduce or pet project you intend to push for? *(Nixon looks absolutely blank)*

NIXON No, nothing in particular. I was elected to smash the labor bosses and my own principle is to accept no dictation from the CIO-PAC.

WASHINGTON *(Reading)* The young Congressman became chairman of the Subcommittee on un-American Activities.

NIXON Politically, it can be the kiss of death.

WASHINGTON He went after Commies.

NIXON *(At large)* Anyone who thinks Communism in this country is just an idea is crazy as hell.

KENNEDY   Let's skip the Hiss case.

NIXON   Like hell we will.

EISENHOWER   That's my boy. *(Alger Hiss flashes on screen)*

WASHINGTON   That "like hell we will" was invented.

NIXON   The tragedy of this case is that men like Alger Hiss who came from good families, are graduates of our best schools, and are awarded the highest honors in government service, find the Communist ideology more attractive than American democracy. *(Whittaker Chambers flashes on screen)* There were rumors that Chambers had spent some time in a mental institution, was insane, was an habitual drunkard and a homosexual . . . it seemed to me that this was a typical Commie tactic . . .

WASHINGTON   Did Alger Hiss, a government official, give secrets to Whittaker Chambers, a one-time, self-admitted Communist agent?

NIXON   Hiss denied ever having heard the name Whittaker Chambers. *(A series of fast shots of the case, headlines, pumpkins, all done rapidly, confusingly)* If the American people understood the real character of Alger, they would boil him in oil. He was rather insolent toward me from the time that I insisted on bringing Frankfurter's name in . . .

HANNAH'S VOICE OVER   Why don't you drop the case, Richard? No one else thinks Hiss is guilty.

NIXON   Although we could not determine who was lying on the issue of whether or not Hiss was a Communist, we should at least go into the matter of whether or not Chambers knew Hiss.

WASHINGTON   Hiss finally admitted he knew Chambers. He was convicted of perjury. And our hero was

(25)

famous. *(TV cameras appear. Nixon unfolds before them)*
NIXON *(Solemnly)*   The nation finally saw that the magnitude of the threat of Communism in the United States is multiplied a thousandfold because of its direct connection with and support by the massive power of the world Communist conspiracy centered in Moscow.
KENNEDY   Oh, boy!
NIXON   Communism in America is part and parcel of Communism abroad. The problem, like Communism itself, is indivisible.
KENNEDY *(Ironically)*   That's telling 'em.
EISENHOWER   So why are we in Vietnam?
WASHINGTON   Shhh. There's some very good stuff coming up.
NIXON   The Communist Hiss believed in an absolutely materialistic view of the world, in principles of deliberate manipulation by a dedicated elite, and in an ideal world society in which the party of the workers replaces God as the prime mover and sole judge of right and wrong.
EISENHOWER *(Envy)*   They never gave *me* speeches like that . . .
NIXON   Folks. Our beliefs must be combined with a crusading zeal not just to hold our own but to change the world—including the Communist world—and to win the battle for freedom, individual dignity, and true economic progress without a hot war.
KENNEDY *(Quite seriously)*   That's why we are in Vietnam.
(Shots of Korea, McCarthy, Truman, MacArthur)
WASHINGTON   Nineteen-fifty. The Korean war has begun. Senator McCarthy is leading a crusade against Communists in government. Yet according to President Truman . . . *(Truman's face flashes on backdrop)*

TRUMAN'S VOICE OVER   Under this administration the position of the United States as a world power has increased . . . *(Nixon has been campaigning again. He stops, shakes his head, scowls)*

NIXON *(Points to Truman)*   That is the most dishonest remark in America's political history. There is no question that we have been losing the cold war. You seriously wonder if a man is qualified to lead this nation after such a statement as he has made. *("The American People" roll toward Nixon)*

JOURNALIST'S VOICE OVER   President Truman, what do you think of Mr. Nixon?

TRUMAN'S VOICE OVER   Son of a bitch. *(Nixon glowers)*

WASHINGTON   Our hero has now decided to run for the Senate against Helen Gahagan Douglas.

VOICE OVER   But in a state where there are more Democrats than Republicans you must appeal to Democrats. So in the primary campaign we sent out a little booklet to all Democrats, with a picture of Dick with a caption which said, "As one Democrat to Another . . ." *(Shot of actual pamphlet flashes on screen)*

EISENHOWER   That's dishonest.

KENNEDY   He's your boy. *(One of Nixon's aides turns to Nixon)*

NIXON'S AIDE   Don't talk about Communism . . . It's been overworked. *(Nixon turns upstage to "The American People")*

NIXON   I have been advised not to talk about Communism; but I am going to tell the people of California the truth, this is one thing we cannot stop talking about as long as the menace of international Communism faces us here in the United States.

(27)

Gore Vidal

WASHINGTON Helen Gahagan Douglas was *not* a Communist. But it was necessary for Nixon to make her seem like one if he was to be elected.

NIXON During the six years she has been in Congress, she has consistently supported the State Department's policy of appeasing Communism in Asia, which finally resulted in the Korean war. *(Enter Mrs. Douglas. She mounts the pedestal at stage right, just as Voorhis did. Nixon climbs onto his pedestal. "The American People" are now at dead center)*

VOICE OVER Her attitude toward Communism is soft. During five years in Congress Helen Douglas voted 353 times exactly as has Vito Marcantonio, the notorious Communist party-line congressman from New York . . . How can Helen Douglas, capable actress that she is, take up so strange a role as a foe of Communism? And why does she, when she has so deservedly earned the title of "The Pink Lady"?

WASHINGTON *(To the audience)* What you have just heard was from some literature distributed by Nixon's campaign manager for Southern California. Mrs. Douglas is now known as The Pink Lady.

HELEN DOUGLAS Although Mr. Nixon is a Republican he voted 112 times the same way Marcantonio did. I voted 85 percent of the time with a majority of either the House or my party. I am not a Communist.

NIXON My opponent did not vote as a Democrat. She did not vote as a Republican. It just so happens that my opponent is a member of a small clique which joins the notorious party-liner Vito Marcantonio of New York, in voting, time after time, against measures that are for the security of this country.

(28)

VOICE OVER   Always repeat your charge. Always attack. The Pink Lady is now on the defensive.

HELEN DOUGLAS   I am against such pipsqueaks as Nixon and McCarthy, who are trying to get us so frightened of Communism that we'll be afraid to turn out the lights at night. (*"The American People" are moving back and forth between the two candidates*) I am fighting a backwash of young men in dark shirts. (*Campaign workers pick up receivers . . . whisper*)

CAMPAIGN WORKERS   This is a friend. Helen Douglas is a Communist. (*"The American People" begin to inch toward Nixon*)

WASHINGTON   From out of state came Senator Joseph McCarthy to speak for Nixon. And denounce the Secretary of State, Dean Acheson. (*McCarthy flashes on screen*)

MCCARTHY'S VOICE OVER   Acheson must go. We cannot fight international atheistic Communism with men who are either traitors or who are hip-deep in their own failures . . . The chips are down between the American people and the Administration's Comicrat Party of Betrayal.

WASHINGTON   Gerald Smith of the Christian Nationalist Crusade also spoke for Nixon. (*Photos of Gerald Smith and supporters*)

GERALD SMITH'S VOICE OVER   The man who uncovered Hiss is in California to do the same housecleaning here. Help Richard Nixon get rid of the Jew Communists.

EISENHOWER (*Alarmed*) I don't think that's a very good way to talk in public . . .

KENNEDY Don't worry. *After* the election, Dick will make it absolutely clear that he's not anti-Semitic.

(*29*)

GERALD SMITH'S VOICE OVER   Helen Douglas is the wife of a Jew. You Californians can do one thing very soon to further the ideals of Christian Nationalism, and that is *not* to send to the Senate the wife of a Jew. (*"The American People" are now lurching toward Nixon. Whispers of "Communist, Jew, Pink Lady," "Communist, Jew, Pink Lady" grow louder. "The American People" are now with Nixon all the way. Mrs. Douglas departs*)

WASHINGTON   Another fighting, rocking, socking campaign paid off. Nixon is now a Senator. (*Applause onstage as Nixon gets off his pedestal. An interviewer accosts him*)

INTERVIEWER   They call you Tricky Dick, Mr. Nixon. Why?

NIXON   This is another typical smear by the same left-wing elements which have fought me ever since I took part in the investigation which led to the conviction of Alger Hiss.

INTERVIEWER   Could it be because you tried to make people believe Mrs. Douglas was a Communist?

NIXON (*Firmly*)   I never said that Helen Douglas was a Communist. I specifically said she was not. I did charge her with a lack of understanding of Communism. Frankly, I had hoped Communism would not be an issue in the campaign.

INTERVIEWER   Liar!

NIXON (*Explodes*)   We'll take care of people like you. Okay, boys, throw him out.

EISENHOWER   I didn't follow domestic . . . uh, politics too much at that period . . .

KENNEDY   Well, get set. You're about to make him Vice President.

EISENHOWER   Not me. That was Tom Dewey's idea. I . . . well, uh, hardly knew Mr. Nixon . . . he did come to Paris to talk to me once . . . seemed a personable young fella . . . but . . .

WASHINGTON   A group of California businessmen put together a fund for Nixon to use in the fight against Socialism. As a result, Nixon was now able—July 5, 1951— to make a down payment on a house in Washington. *(The house, then the deed appear on screen)* Nixon signed a lease, agreeing that he would never *(Washington squints at the deed and reads actual text)* "sell, lease or rent th e property to anyone of negro blood, or any person of the semitic race which includes Armenians, Jews, Hebrews, Persians and Syrians."

KENNEDY   What about Arabs?

WASHINGTON   Our hero spoke out fearlessly on the subject of the war in Korea. He supported General MacArthur who had just been dismissed for wanting to expand the war. *(On screen: MacArthur's royal progress in New York after Truman fired him)*

NIXON *(To the audience)*   There are only two alternatives to MacArthur's policy: continuing the Korean war without any real hope of winning it, or ending it with a political settlement . . . The only political settlement possible would amount to appeasement . . . what the Chinese communists insist upon is a seat in the United Nations and control of Formosa—laying the foundation for eventual Communist domination of all Asia and in the end an inevitable world war.

EISENHOWER *(To Kennedy)*   Did I hear somewhere that he's planning to go to Peking?

(31)

KENNEDY   Yes. And I'll bet he never gets there. It's like you and Moscow.

EISENHOWER   Damn fool thing to do . . .

INTERVIEWER *(To Nixon)*   Do you believe the rumors that there is a split between China and the Soviet?

NIXON   Wishful thinking. I believe they are partners with the same major objectives.

WASHINGTON   On July 11, 1952, the most beloved hero in the nation's history . . . Dwight Eisenhower . . . *(Washington's reading is on the order of Sonny Tufts!)* . . .was nominated for President. *(Riotous cheering in which Eisenhower absently joins)*

KENNEDY   It's you. You're on.

EISENHOWER   Back to life?

KENNEDY   That's what they call it. *(Eisenhower goes to center stage, puts on his Eisenhower mask, raises his arms, grins broadly. Everyone onstage applauds. Nixon jumps up and down excitedly. Then the smile stops, and we are in a policy meeting of Republicans. Eisenhower looks grim)*

REPUBLICAN 1   He's young . . .

REPUBLICAN 2   Too young . . .

EISENHOWER   He's forty-two . . .

REPUBLICAN 1   Thirty-nine.

EISENHOWER   That's what I said.

REPUBLICAN 3   And he's from California . . . Good balance to the ticket . . . We want him, General.

EISENHOWER   So it's Nick Dixon?

REPUBLICAN 3 *(Spells it out carefully)*   No, General, Dick Nixon. He's your running mate. For Vice President. Of the United States. Of America.

EISENHOWER   What'll I say about him? *(A paper is given him. Lights go up. Nixon and Eisenhower cross to down center stage, arms raised, beaming. It is the nominating convention. Typical music. Then Eisenhower reads haltingly . . .)* A man who has shown statesmanlike qualities in many ways, but has a special talent and an ability to ferret out any kind of subversive influence wherever it may be found and the strength and persistence to get rid of it.

NIXON *(To audience)* Folks! Haven't we got a wonderful candidate for President of the United States? *(The two walk away. Eisenhower is all business. Dismisses Nixon, who acts as if he wants to tag along. Eisenhower then removes his mask and rejoins Kennedy and Washington. Nixon addresses the audience)* Despite Ike's great capacity for friendliness, he also had a quality of reserve which at least subconsciously tended to make a visitor feel like a junior officer coming in to see the commanding General.

KENNEDY My own impression.

EISENHOWER *(Serenely)* Well, I *am* a commanding General and you two are junior officers. *(Eisenhower and Kennedy go offstage)*

WASHINGTON Now another fighting, rocking, socking campaign is under way.

NIXON'S VOICE OVER There has never been any doubt in my mind about Mr. Truman's complete loyalty to the country but . . . *(Nixon is now darting around the stage as usual, campaigning—shaking hands, smiling, waving)* The plan was for General Eisenhower to stress the positive aspects of his crusade to clean up the mess in Washington. I was to hammer away at our opponents on the record of the Truman administration, with particular emphasis on Communist subversion. *(Adlai Stevenson enters—wearing his mask—and takes his place on the stage-right pedestal. Masked, Eisenhower takes his place on the opposite pedestal. Eisenhower*

(33)

*is benign, not listening. Nixon stands at the foot of Eisen-
hower's pedestal)*

NIXON *(Points)* There he is! Adlai Stevenson! Adlai the Appeaser who got a Ph.D. from Dean Acheson's College of Cowardly Communist Containment.

STEVENSON This brash young man who aspires to the Vice Presidency . . .

NIXON Mr. Stevenson was a character witness for Alger Hiss . . . at a time when he was governor of Illinois and the prestige of a great state was thrown in behalf of the defendant . . . it is significant that Mr. Stevenson has never expressed any indignation over what Mr. Hiss has done and the treachery that he engaged in against his country.

WASHINGTON Treachery? But he was convicted of perjury, not treason. . .

NIXON *(Ignores this)* Let me emphasize that there is no question in my mind as to the loyalty of Mr. Stevenson, but the question is one as to his judgment . . .

STEVENSON Alger Hiss, General Eisenhower, John Foster Dulles were all on the board together of Carnegie Endowment. Mr. Dulles said, quote, "there is no reason to doubt Mr. Hiss's complete loyalty to our American institutions," unquote. I bring these facts to the American people . . .

NIXON Mr. Truman, Secretary Acheson and Governor Stevenson are traitors to the high principles in which many of the nation's Democrats believe. Real Democrats are outraged by the Truman-Acheson-Stevenson gang's toleration of Communism in high places.

STEVENSON *(Over Nixon)* I mention these facts not to suggest that either Eisenhower or Dulles are soft toward Communism or even guilty of bad judgment . . .

(34)

NIXON   He will drive the American economy farther left-ward in the direction of ruinous Socialism.

STEVENSON   . . . but only to make the point that the mistrust, the innuendos, the accusations which this "Crusade" is employing, threaten not merely themselves, but the integrity of our institutions.

NIXON *(To the audience)*   I had hoped frankly that Communist subversion in the United States would *not* be an issue in the campaign. *(A heckler steps forward)*

HECKLER   What about your sixteen-thousand-dollar slush fund? *(A deadly hush onstage; everyone freezes. Nixon looks poleaxed. Then Eisenhower steps off his pedestal and exits. Stevenson does the same. Except for Kennedy and Washington, Nixon is alone with the heckler)* Tell us about the sixteen-thousand-dollars.

NIXON *(Automatically)*   You folks know I did the work of investigating the Communists in the United States. Ever since I have done that work, the Communists and the leftwingers have been fighting me with every smear . . . (The heckler, smiling, goes)

CHOTINER'S VOICE OVER   When your candidate is under attack, don't answer until the opposition has exhausted its ammunition. When you answer it, do so with an attack of your own against the opposition for having launched it in the first place. *(Interviewer and Dana Smith, California businessman, enter)*

INTERVIEWER   You are Mr. Dana Smith, one of the contributors to Senator Nixon's fund. How much did you give him?

SMITH   Between the time of his election to the Senate and his nomination as Vice President we gave him be-

(35)

tween sixteen and seventeen thousand dollars which I disbursed.

WASHINGTON   The sum was actually *eighteen* thousand dollars.

INTERVIEWER   Why did you give him the money?

SMITH   Dick seemed to be the best salesman against socialization available. We realized that his salary was pitifully inadequate. . . . he told us he needed money for such things as long distance phone calls, for ten thousand Christmas cards, for . . .

INTERVIEWER   But what did he *do* for any of you? Did he help you get contracts from the government? (*Mr. Dana Smith has vanished. As the masked Eisenhower enters with journalists, Washington consults document*)

WASHINGTON   According to Nixon the fund was used for expenses which he did not want the taxpayers to assume. He also said that he never used his office as Senator to help the contributors.

JOURNALIST   The newsmen on the train have taken a vote. They think you should drop Nixon. (*Eisenhower looks firm*)

EISENHOWER   I'm taking my time on this. Nothing's decided, contrary to your idea that this is all a setup for a whitewash of Nixon. Nixon has got to be clean as a hound's tooth. (*Eisenhower and entourage go off. Nixon is now surrounded by his own entourage*)

NIXON   (*Exploding*)   Clean as a hound's tooth! (*He is about to let fly a volley of four-letter words, when he recalls the audience is watching. With an effort, he controls himself. To the audience*) Our little group was somewhat dismayed by reports of Eisenhower's attitude. I must admit it made me feel like the little boy caught with jam on his face.

CHOTINER'S VOICE OVER   How stupid can they be? If these damned amateurs around Eisenhower just had the sense they were born with they would recognize that this is a purely political attack . . .

AIDE   The New York *Herald-Tribune* and the Washington *Post* want you to get off the ticket. *(A telephone rings. An aide answers)* It's General Eisenhower. *(Nixon leaps at the telephone, grabs it to him)*

EISENHOWER'S VOICE   I think you ought to go on a nationwide television program and tell them everything there is to tell, everything you can remember since the day you entered public life.

NIXON   General, do I have your endorsement now?

EISENHOWER'S VOICE   If I issue a statement now, backing you up, in effect people will accuse me of condoning wrongdoing.

NIXON   General, do you think *after* the television program that an announcement could then be made one way or the other?

EISENHOWER'S VOICE   I am hoping that no announcement would be necessary at all, but maybe after the program we could tell what ought to be done.

NIXON   I know how difficult this problem is for you, but there comes a time when you either piss or get off the pot. *(A click on the other end of the line. Nixon glowers. Meanwhile aides set up a television studio. Two chairs. Pat sits in one. Nixon sits in the other. Lights go up. Trial run. An aide approaches)*

AIDE   Governor Dewey, with Eisenhower. On the phone. *(Nixon crosses to the telephone)*

DEWEY'S VOICE   There has been a meeting of all of Eisenhower's top advisers. They have asked me to tell you that

(37)

it is their opinion that at the conclusion of the broadcast tonight you should submit your resignation to Eisenhower. *(Nixon, stunned, speaks in a very low voice into the receiver. We cannot hear him)*

DEWEY'S VOICE   Can I say you have accepted?

NIXON   You will have to watch the show to see—and tell them I know something about politics, too. *(Nixon hangs up. As he is about to return to his seat, an aide brings him a telegram)*

AIDE   From your mother. *(As Nixon opens the telegram, we hear Hannah's voice)*

HANNAH'S VOICE OVER   We are thinking of you. *(For a moment Nixon genuinely weeps; then he marches into the TV studio, sits down. Eisenhower and his aides are at the opposite end of the stage watching a television set. Eisenhower is seated, a pad on his knee, a pencil in hand. A technician gives a signal. Since we cannot give the full thirty-minute drama, musical bridges are used between points: some are patriotic—"It's a Grand Old Flag"—some are hearts and flowers . . . a full emotional medley)*

NIXON   My fellow Americans, I come before you tonight as a candidate for the Vice Presidency and as a man whose honesty and integrity have been questioned. *(Musical bridge)*

I went to the South Pacific. I guess I'm entitled to a couple of battle stars. I got a couple of letters of commendation but I was just there when the bombs were falling. *(Musical bridge. On the screen—a confusion of mortgages, bankbooks, old clothes, a house)*

Well, that's what we have. And that's what we own. It isn't very much . . . I should say this, that Pat doesn't have a mink coat. But she does have a respectable Republican

(38)

cloth coat, and I always tell her that she would look good in anything. *(Musical bridge)*

We did get something, a gift after the nomination. A man down in Texas heard Pat on the radio mention the fact that our two youngsters would like to have a dog and, believe it or not, the day before we left on this campaign trip we got a message from Union Station in Baltimore, saying they had a package for us. We went down to get it. You know what it was? It was a little cocker spaniel dog . . . *(A huge portrait of Checkers wreathed in flowers appears on screen)*

. . . in a crate that he had sent all the way from Texas— black and white, spotted, and our little girl, Tricia, the six-year-old, named it Checkers. And you know, the kids, like all kids, loved the dog, and I just want to say this, right now, that regardless of what they say about it, we are going to keep it. *(Musical bridge. Several of those around Eisenhower are openly weeping; he is not)*

I believe that it's fine that a man like Governor Stevenson who inherited a fortune from his father can run for President. But I also feel that it is essential in this country of ours that a man of modest means can also run for President. *(Musical bridge)*

You have read in the papers about other funds. Now, Mr. Stevenson apparently had a couple—one of them in which a group of business people paid and helped to supplement the salaries of state employees. Here is where the money went directly into their pockets. I think what Mr. Stevenson should do is come before the American people, as I have . . . *(Musical bridge. Aides are staring at Eisenhower, who looks as if he is about to have a stroke)*

(39)

AIDE   General, you will have to declare *your* income, too. *(Eisenhower says nothing: he has got the point)*

NIXON   Wire and write the Republican National Committee whether you think I should stay or whether I should get off. *(Consternation among the Eisenhower aides. The General breaks the pencil. This is the wrong scenario)*

And whatever their decision is I will abide by it. And remember, folks, Eisenhower is a great man. Folks, he is a great man and a vote for Eisenhower is a vote for what is good for America. *(Technician gestures: Nixon is off the air. He is distraught)*

I'm off? But I didn't give the address of the National Committee! *(In a rage Nixon throws cue cards to the floor)*

CHOTINER'S VOICE OVER   A triumph. May I suggest to you that I think that the classic that will live in all political history came on September twenty-third nineteen-fifty-two, from Los Angeles, California, when the candidate for the Vice Presidency answered, if you please, with an attack against those who had made one on him.

NIXON   I was an utter flop. *(Pat and he start offstage as Eisenhower and aides move to center stage. Bitterly)* At least we got the dog vote tonight. *(Exeunt Pat and Nixon)*

AIDE   General, that audience out there saw the same show. They'll want your reaction. *(Eisenhower nods grimly. Then he steps onto a pedestal. Arms raised to cheers)*

EISENHOWER   I like courage . . . tonight I saw an example of courage . . . I have never seen anyone come through in such a fashion as Senator Nixon did tonight . . . When I get in a fight I would rather have a courageous and honest man by my side than a whole boxcar full of pussyfooters. *(Loud applause)*But . . . it is obvious that I have to have something more than one single presentation, necessarily

limited to thirty minutes, the time allowed Senator Nixon
. . . (*Scene shifts. Eisenhower joins aides at one end of the stage,
waiting for a plane to arrive*)

WASHINGTON (*Reads*) After a good deal of—farting
around, Eisenhower decides to keep Nixon on the
ticket. They meet at the airport in Wheeling, West
Virginia. (*Nixon and Pat appear, haggard. Flash bulbs go
off*)

NIXON General, you didn't need to come to the airport.

EISENHOWER Why not? You're my boy.

WASHINGTON So moved was our hero by the applause
and the cheers that he broke down and wept on the
shoulder of Senator Knowland. (*Nixon breaks down,
weeps on the shoulder of Senator Knowland as flash bulbs go
off. "The American People" are crowding him and Ike . . . A
landslide is building. Kennedy has reappeared; crosses to
Washington. He looks with contempt at the happy warriors*)

KENNEDY Tasteless . . .

WASHINGTON (*Shakes his head*) Deeply American. In-
spiring. (*Nixon is now campaigning triumphantly*)

KENNEDY Come off it. First, Nixon says he took the
money so that the taxpayers wouldn't have to pay for
his expenses. That's not true. They could not have
paid those expenses even if he wanted them to. Then
he said he did nothing for those fat cats who gave him
the money. That's a lie. His office rang up the Justice
Department on behalf of Dana Smith and asked for a
half-million-dollar tax rebate. Then he said none of
the money went for his personal use. Another lie. He
told Peter Edson, the journalist, that he could not have
made the down payment on his house in Washington
without the fund . . .

(*41*)

NIXON'S VOICE OVER   It isn't what the facts are but what they *appear* to be that counts when you are under fire in a political campaign. *(Nixon is stopped by an interviewer)*

INTERVIEWER   In dealing with pensions for the old and handicapped . . .

NIXON   I am opposed to pensions in any form, as it makes loafing more attractive than working.

INTERVIEWER   What about Governor Stevenson's plan to end the Korean war?

NIXON   If Mr. Stevenson or anyone else in the Truman administration has a plan to end the war, it should be put into effect now.

VOICE OVER   It is now October, one month before elections.

NIXON *(A cry)*   There is only one month left to save America! *(White House, Capitol, Inauguration on screen. "Hail to the Chief")*

WASHINGTON   Eisenhower and Nixon are elected, and Eisenhower ends the war the Democrats started in Korea. The golden days of Eisenhower the Good have begun. *(Eisenhower appears with a caddy. He begins putting happily. Nixon starts darting about shaking hands)* Nixon gets ready for the congressional elections of 1954. His favorite theme is still Communism. *(An interviewer approaches Nixon)*

INTERVIEWER   Mr. Vice President, do you believe we should come to the aid of the French in Vietnam?

NIXON   If in order to avoid further Communistic expansion in Asia and particularly in Indo-China, if in order to avoid it we must take the risk *now* by putting American boys in, I believe that the Executive branch of the government has to take the politically unpopular position of facing up to it and doing it, and I personally would support such a decision . . . (*Eisenhower has heard this; he looks up, face full of wrath*)

EISENHOWER I would never send troops there. (*The interviewer deserts the chastened Nixon for Eisenhower*)

INTERVIEWER But do we have troops in Vietnam? already?

EISENHOWER The United States has . . . uh, military missions in Indo-China. Yes.

INTERVIEWER Then you agree with the Vice President that if the French should fail, we will go in?

EISENHOWER I can conceive of no greater tragedy than for the United States to become involved in an all-out war in Indo-China.

WASHINGTON Bad news continues from Indo-China. The French are defeated. (*Shots of the French defeat in Vietnam*)

NIXON It is hoped that the United States will not have to send troops there, but if this government cannot avoid it (*A nervous glance at Eisenhower*) the administration must face up to the situation and dispatch forces. (*Eisenhower is now purple with fury*)

EISENHOWER We would not get into a war except through constitutional process, which of course involves the declaration of war by Congress.

INTERVIEWER Then you agree with the Vice President that we are in danger of losing Indo-China the way we lost China?

EISENHOWER (*Reluctantly*) The loss of Indo-China *would* lead to the loss of Burma, Thailand, in fact all of the great peninsula on which they are situated. (*Nixon is delighted by the admission*)

INTERVIEWER   Mr. President, do you favor sending in American combat troops?

EISENHOWER *(A pause)*   No.

WASHINGTON   Our hero campaigned hard in 1954 to elect a Republican Congress. *(Nixon starts campaigning again as Eisenhower continues with his golf)*

NIXON'S VOICE OVER   Unfortunately, for our side, there are no great national issues this year. *(Nixon mounts his pedestal. "The American People" have been wheeled onstage)*

NIXON   The issue is the inexcusable actions of a few leaders of the previous administration, who by underestimating the danger of Communist infiltration, by ignoring the warnings of J. Edgar Hoover and the FBI . . . *(To Nixon's surprise, "The American People" start to edge away from him. He stops. Starts again. A new tack)* When the Eisenhower administration came to Washington on January 20, 1953, we found in the files a blueprint for socializing America. *("The American People" show a bit of interest. Edge back. Nixon smiles)*

This dangerous, well-oiled scheme contained plans for adding 40 billion to the national debt by 1956. It called for socialized medicine, socialized agriculture, socialized water and power. *("The American People" start edging away. Nixon is in trouble. He cries) Why* is the Communist Party of the United States fighting so desperately and openly for the defeat of Republican candidates for the House and Senate . . .? *("The American People" stop; but don't edge back. On the screen is flashed the statistic: "Members of American Communist Party, 1954: 20,000 excluding FBI")*

The Communist Party in America is right in one respect

when it says: The 1954 elections are crucial in determining the path America will take. It has determined to conduct its program within the *Democratic* Party. (*"The American People" are heading for the exit*)

Mr. Stevenson has been guilty, probably without being aware that he was doing so, of spreading pro-Communist propaganda . . . (*Desperately*) Ninety-six percent of the 6,926 Communists, fellow travelers, sex perverts, people with criminal records, dope addicts, drunks and other security risks removed under the Eisenhower security program were hired by the Truman administration. (*"The American People" have vanished. Nixon fishes in his pocket, withdraws paper*)

There has come into my possession a copy of a secret memorandum which was sent to Communist Party leaders in California . . . (*But the game is up. Eisenhower sinks a putt, grins at Nixon maliciously. Defeated, Nixon steps off the pedestal. An interviewer approaches*)

INTERVIEWER   You have been accused of smearing as disloyal leaders of the Democratic Party . . .

NIXON   If there was any smearing done in this campaign, their record has done it. They made it, we did not. To put it bluntly, they smeared themselves.

INTERVIEWER   What about Vietnam?

NIXON   The Vietnamese lack the ability to conduct a war by themselves or govern themselves.

INTERVIEWER   What do you think of the Supreme Court's decision to desegregate the schools?

NIXON   There could be an honest disagreement as to whether: first, the Court had the power to do what it did; second, whether it was wise to do what it did; third, whether it should have done it when it was overturning a decision that it previously made.

WASHINGTON Our hero was given full credit for Republican losses that year. *(In the background, Eisenhower suddenly holds his chest; goes offstage. An aide rushes up to Nixon)*

AIDE The President has had a coronary!

NIXON Oh, my God. *(Reporters surround him. Haltingly)* I find it rather difficult to express, in words, feelings that are deep.

WASHINGTON But Eisenhower recovered. Naturally, there was talk that Eisenhower would not run again. That Nixon would. *(Nixon looks eager; statesmanlike. He is confronted with a reporter)*

REPORTER Will your Navy Day speech at San Diego be political?

NIXON My speech will not be political.

REPORTER Will it contain criticism of Democrats?

NIXON I never criticize Democrats.

REPORTER Will you criticize the Democratic leadership?

NIXON *(Rattled)* Do you want your questions answered? Then be quiet.

WASHINGTON But from California came word from his old friend Senator Knowland.

KNOWLAND'S VOICE OVER I do not consider a Pepsodent smile, a ready quip, and an actor's perfection with lines, nor an ability to avoid issues, as qualifications for high office. *(Nixon visibly shrinks)*

WASHINGTON Eisenhower ran again. *(Eisenhower returns, waving happily)*

REPORTER Mr. President, will Nixon be your running mate?

(46)

EISENHOWER   Well, Dick's a fine young fellow, but maybe it would be better if he took a Cabinet job. *(Nixon looks very hurt)*

WASHINGTON   Harold Stassen tried to dump him. *(Eisenhower clutches his stomach and hurries offstage)* The President has just had an ileitis attack. *(On screen, charts of Eisenhower's stomach)* It was important that there be a Vice President of sufficient stature to succeed.

NIXON   I informed the President . . . I would be honored to accept the nomination again . . .

AIDE'S VOICE OVER   The President has asked me to tell you gentlemen that he was delighted to hear of the Vice President's decision. *(Eisenhower appears and takes his position on the pedestal. Stevenson ascends his pedestal. Nixon takes up a position beneath the smiling Eisenhower)*

NIXON   The party of Schlesinger, Stevenson and Bowles is a far cry from the party of Jefferson and Wilson. *("The American People" edge toward Stevenson)*

STEVENSON   I favor stopping the explosions of nuclear weapons in the atmosphere.

NIXON   The Russian prime minister has enthusiastically endorsed Mr. Stevenson's plan. We all realize that these plans were reached independently. *(Those onstage laugh. Grimly)* I am not saying that facetiously.

STEVENSON   Nixon is simply Joe McCarthy in a white collar.

NIXON   What Mr. Stevenson calls me is unimportant but I resent his typically snide and snobbish innuendo towards the millions of Americans who work for a living in our shops and factories.

STEVENSON   Welcome to Nixon-land—a land of slander and smear, of sly innuendo, of the poison pen, the anony-

(47)

mous phone call and hustling, pushing, shoving—the land of smash and grab—anything to win. (*"The American People" are lining up with Stevenson. Suddenly Eisenhower raises his arms*)

EISENHOWER   My fellow Americans . . . (*"The American People" hurtle toward him; he has won again*)

WASHINGTON   Eisenhower and Nixon were reelected. There was talk of a new Nixon. His attacks had been milder than usual. There were times when he seemed to doubt that Adlai Stevenson was a Communist.

NIXON   But you don't win campaigns with a diet of dishwater and milk toast.

WASHINGTON   A month after the election, on December 10, 1956. Nixon's mother Hannah was loaned $205,000 by a Mr. Frank Waters, representing the industrialist Howard Hughes. As collateral for the loan Mrs. Nixon gave the trust deed on a lot she owned in Whittier, valued at $13,000. Hannah then turned over to her son Donald's company $165,000. This way, there was no public record of any transaction between Hughes Tool and Nixon's brother Donald. (*During this, Hannah and Waters and Donald Nixon are onstage, passing checks, surreptitiously, back and forth. Thoughtfully, Nixon observes this ballet. As an interviewer enters, all flee but Nixon*)

INTERVIEWER   Could you explain to us the loan Howard Hughes made to your brother, Donald?

NIXON   It seems to me that the troubles of a man's family are, frankly, none of the public's business . . . (*Eisenhower clutches his head and goes offstage. The screen fills with sputnik, Adams, rug, U 2, etc.*)

(*48*)

WASHINGTON Eisenhower has had a stroke. Troubles begin for the administration and the country. The Russians go into space with sputnik, Sherman Adams takes a rug from a lobbyist. Nixon goes to Caracas with Pat. A good-will tour Nixon-style. *(Nixon and Pat face a hostile crowd)*

NIXON'S VOICE OVER This was not my first experience in facing a Communist-led gang. *(Pat and Dick move slowly, apprehensively, as the mob shouts "Muera Nixon!")* Take the offensive. Show no fear. Do the unexpected but do nothing rash. I felt the excitement of battle as I spoke but I had full control of my temper as I lashed out at the mob.

NIXON *(Shouts)* You are cowards, you are afraid of the truth! You are the worst kind of cowards! *(Nixon and Pat duck into a mock-automobile. The automobile moves to the opposite end of the stage. Mob pounds on it. Car stops. Nixon gets out. A guard holds back the mob. Pat scuttles offstage. Nixon pauses. Man approaches. Guard blocks him)*

NIXON'S VOICE OVER I saw before me a weird-looking character whose bulging eyes seemed to merge with his mouth and nose in one distorted blob. He let fly a wad of spit which caught me full in the face. *(Nixon wipes his face)* I felt an almost uncontrollable desire, urge, to tear the face in front of me to pieces. *(The guard has started to drag the man off)* As I saw his legs go by, I at least had the satisfaction of planting a healthy kick on his shins. *(Nixon kicks the man's shins)* Nothing I did all day made me feel better. *(Nixon proudly exits. Washington comes downstage)*

WASHINGTON Nixon gained in popularity as a result of having been attacked in Caracas. *(To the audience)* Don't ask me why. *(Nixon has now reentered. He comes downstage and gravely addresses the audience)*

(49)

NIXON   Not all the rioters of course were Communists. But this misses the major point. There can be no doubt that the riots were Communist-planned, Communist-led and Communist-controlled.

INTERVIEWER   Are you pleased with the administration's record in Vietnam?

NIXON *(Nods)* Through the courage of President Diem and timely American aid, freedom was not only returned them, but the people have obtained the best rule in their - history.

INTERVIEWER   Looking back on your Pink Lady campaign for the Senate against Mrs. Douglas, what do you think now?

NIXON   I'm sorry about that episode. I was a very young man. *(Nixon now darts about the stage, campaigning, as always)*

WASHINGTON   The 1958 congressional campaign was a disaster for the Republicans and for the new Nixon. In October just before the election, he said . . .

NIXON   As far as our candidates are concerned, they are the best men for the jobs in every office that they seek.

WASHINGTON   In November, just after the election, he said . . .

NIXON   This year our crop of candidates was one of the poorest since I entered public life.

WASHINGTON   But there were triumphs to come. At an exhibition American kitchen in Moscow, our hero faced Khrushchev himself. *(Nixon stands beside a stove which has just been rolled onstage. Khrushchev is opposite him, wearing a mask. An interpreter is in between. Nixon turns to the audience)*

(50)

NIXON   Never before had a head of government met me with a tirade of four-letter words which made his inter-preter blush as he translated them into English. *(Nixon shakes his head with horror; rejoins Khrushchev, who is spouting Russian. Cameras turn)* You must not be afraid of ideas. After all, you don't know everything . . . *(Exchange in Russian)*

INTERPRETER *(To Nixon)*   The Chairman says: if I don't know everything, you don't know anything about Communism—except fear of it.

NIXON *(Soothingly)*   There are some instances where you may be ahead of us. For example, in the thrust of your rockets for the investigation of outer space. *(Nixon looks suddenly aggressive; eyes make sure that cameramen are ready for a shot. Then he waggles his forefinger sternly under Khrushchev's nose)* There may be some instances in which we are ahead of you—in color television, for instance. *(The delighted cameramen get this picture of Nixon being tough with Khrushchev, who is furious. A torrent of Russian)*

INTERPRETER   He says you are a slick lawyer while he is a simple man of the people, a coal miner . . .

NIXON   You may be interested to know that my father owned a small general store in California and all the Nixon boys worked there while going to school. *(A moment while this is translated)*

INTERPRETER   The Chairman says all shopkeepers are thieves. *(The scene breaks up. Nixon faces the audience)*

NIXON   Later I wished I'd said, yes, but there is honor among thieves.

WASHINGTON   As a result of this encounter, our hero's stock goes up. Which was a good thing, for the age of Eisenhower is drawing to a close. Castro is in Cuba.

An economic recession has begun. Nixon is now maneuvering to be the Republican candidate, the heir of Eisenhower. *(Eisenhower appears with a colleague)*

EISENHOWER   You know, Dick has matured.

COLLEAGUE   What kind of President would he make?

EISENHOWER   He isn't the sort of person you turn to when you want a new idea, but he has a . . . uh, an uncanny ability to draw upon others. *(Exeunt Eisenhower and colleague)*

INTERVIEWER   What is the administration's stand on the integration of black and white?

NIXON   It has not been, is not now, should not be immediate total integration. We have to deal with the facts of life as they are.

INTERVIEWER   What is your view of the role of television in the coming election?

NIXON   Television is not so effective now as it was in 1952. The novelty has worn off.

INTERVIEWER   How do you see yourself?

NIXON   You know, nobody will believe it, but I'm really an egghead.

WASHINGTON   Wednesday, July 27, 1960, Nixon arrived at Chicago, ready to be nominated for President. *(Nixon joins a group of Party leaders)*

LEADER   You can say all you want about foreign affairs, but what's really important is the price of hogs in Chicago and St. Louis.

NIXON   If you ever let the Democrats campaign only on domestic issues, they'll beat us. Our only hope is to keep it on foreign policy. *(Convention music sounds. Nixon starts downstage center)*

INTERVIEWER   Have you put a lot of work into your acceptance speech?

NIXON   Yes, I have spent two weeks reading history, literature and philosophy. *(He is joined by Pat. Then the two daughters are rolled into view: large cutie-pie dolls, on wheels)* To stand here before this great convention, to hear your expression of affection for me, for Pat, for our daughters, for my mother, is of course the greatest moment of my life. *(They freeze in an attitude of glory)*

WASHINGTON   Running against him was the rich young Senator from Massachusetts. A Roman Catholic who had easily defeated Hubert Humphrey in the primaries.

KENNEDY'S VOICE OVER   The times are too grave, the challenge too urgent, the stakes too high to permit the customary passions of political debate. We are not here to curse the darkness, but to light a candle . . . *(The Nixons unfreeze. Nixon crosses to the pedestal where Eisenhower had stood; mounts it. Pat stands beneath, a doll on either side; Kennedy, wearing a mask, enters and takes his place on the opposite pedestal. "The American People" are rolled into view, equidistant between the candidates)*

NIXON *(On the offensive)*   I have no doubt whatever about Senator Kennedy's loyalty to his country . . . *("The American People" start to edge toward Kennedy. Nixon notices this. He also remembers that he is the new Nixon)*

I say that just as in 1952 and 1956 millions of Democrats will join us not because they are deserting their party but because their party deserted them.

KENNEDY *(Refers back to Nixon's opening)*   If my church attempted to influence me in a way which was improper or which affected adversely my responsibilities as public

(53)

servant, sworn to uphold the Constitution, then I would reply to them that this was an improper action on their part . . .

NIXON   I don't believe there is a *religious* issue as far as Senator Kennedy is concerned . . . it would be tragic for this election to be determined, primarily, or even substantially on *religious* grounds . . . the question is not whether Senator Kennedy or I believe that *religion* is an issue—we don't believe it is . . . (*"The American People" are beginning to slide imperceptibly to Nixon; his darting eyes take this in; he becomes even more solemn*)

The question is how do you keep *religion* out of a campaign? The best way is by not talking about it . . . I have issued orders to all of the people in my campaign not to discuss *religion* . . . and as far as I'm concerned, I will decline to *dis*cuss *religion* . . . (*Eisenhower drifts into view with a golf club. An interviewer approaches him*)

INTERVIEWER   What major decisions of your administration has the Vice President participated in?

EISENHOWER   If you give me a week, I might think of one. (*Exeunt Eisenhower and interviewer*)

NIXON   (*Gulping*)   The President was probably being facetious.

REPORTER   What do you think of adding to Social Security a health plan for the aged?

NIXON   (*Shakes his head*)   Inevitably, this would lead in the direction of herding the ill and elderly into institutions whether they desired this or not.

KENNEDY   (*Suddenly*)   The forces fighting for freedom in exile and in the mountains of Cuba should be sustained and assisted. (*Nixon's mouth drops open. "The American*

People" move toward Kennedy. Shots of Castro and Che on the screen. Guerrillas arming)

NIXON'S VOICE OVER   For the first and only time in the campaign I got mad at Kennedy personally. Allen Dulles had briefed Kennedy on the fact that for months the CIA had not only been supporting and assisting but actually training Cuban exiles for the eventual purpose of supporting an invasion of Cuba itself. There was only one thing I coulddo:ImustattacktheKennedyproposal.

WASHINGTON   But why? If you want to invade Cuba, too, then . . .

NIXON *(Through him)*   We would lose all our friends in Latin America, we would probably be condemned in the United Nations, and we would not accomplish our objective . . . it would be an open invitation for Mr. Khrushchev to come into Latin America and to engage us in what would be a civil war and possibly even worse than that . . . *(Washington, puzzled, intervenes)*

WASHINGTON   But, when you said that, you were actually in favor of an invasion of Cuba.

NIXON   Absolutely.

WASHINGTON   Then you lied when you said you opposed Senator Kennedy's plan to assist the enemies of Castro.

NIXON   The covert operation *had* to be protected at all costs. I must not even suggest by implication that the United States was rendering aid to rebel forces in and out of Cuba . . . *(Washington shakes his head. Nixon turns to "The American People")* Folks, Jack Kennedy is going to raise the price of everything you buy in the stores by twenty-five percent.

(55)

WASHINGTON   Certain Democrats were eager to bring up the subject of the Howard Hughes loan to Nixon's brother. But certain Republicans said that if they did, Kennedy's love life would become an issue. A balance of terror was achieved.

NIXON   I draw the line on anything that has to do with the personal life of the candidate.

WASHINGTON *(Facing the audience)*   There were four television debates between the candidates. *(Nixon and Kennedy get off the pedestals. They meet before a TV camera. Smilingly, they shake hands. Then Nixon sees a still photographer ready for a shot. Nixon suddenly puts his forefinger under Kennedy's nose—the way he'd done with Khrushchev)*

NIXON *(To Kennedy)*   And how is Jackie?*(The photographer gets his picture. Kennedy is disgusted. They line up side by side before the TV camera)*

WASHINGTON   Great issues were discussed in the course of the four debates.

KENNEDY   Quemoy.

NIXON   Matsu.

KENNEDY   Matsu.

NIXON   Quemoy . . . *(They babble back and forth, building to "Quemoy and Matsu," "Matsu and Quemoy . . .")*

WASHINGTON   It was generally agreed that Kennedy had looked better on television. Luckily, for the candidates, no one actually listened to either of them.

NIXON *(To the audience)*   Joint TV debate appearances of candidates at the presidential level are here to stay, mainly because people want them and the candidates have a responsibility to inform the public . . .

INTERVIEWER'S VOICE OVER   Mr. Truman, did you ever call Mr. Nixon a son of a bitch?

TRUMAN'S VOICE OVER   How could I? He claims to be a self-made man.

NIXON   I can only say that I'm very proud that President Eisenhower restored dignity and decency and, frankly, good language to the conduct of the Presidency.

WASHINGTON   The election was close. At the last moment Nixon called on Eisenhower for aid. *(Eisenhower appears on a golf buggy, hands upraised, beaming)* Eisenhower almost did the trick. But Kennedy won, narrowly. *(Although "The American People" have been inching toward Nixon, a hair's-breadth remains this side of Kennedy. Nixon crumples. In a daze he gets off the pedestal. Pat weeps. Upstage, Eisenhower continues his golf)*

INTERVIEWER   Well?

NIXON   My little daughter Tricia says she doesn't blame the people who voted for Kennedy, she blames the ones who counted the votes in Chicago.

WASHINGTON   The President-elect met with Nixon in Florida. *(Kennedy graciously shakes Nixon's limp hand)*

NIXON'S VOICE OVER   I brought up an issue which I told him was one on which I had particularly strong views: the recognition of Red China. Admitting Red China to the United Nations would be a mockery of the provisions of the charter, which limits its membership to peace-loving nations. It would give respectability to the Communist regime which would immensely increase its power and prestige in Asia and probably irreparably weaken the non-Communist governments in that area. *(Kennedy in triumph comes to center stage. Nixon, Eisenhower—everyone gathers around. It is the Inaugural Address)*

WASHINGTON   The day of the Inaugural there was a lot of snow. After eight years of Eisenhower's keeping the

(57)

Gore Vidal

peace, the American people were ready—so Kennedy thought—for military adventures of the sort I warned against when I ceased to be First Magistrate nearly two hundred years ago.

KENNEDY   Let the word go forth from this time and place, to friend and foe alike, that the torch has been passed to a new generation of Americans—born in this century, tempered by war, disciplined by a hard and bitter peace . . . proud of our ancient heritage—and unwilling to witness or permit the slow undoing of those human rights to which this nation has always been committed, and to which we are committed today at home and around the world. Let every nation know, whether it wishes us well or ill, that we shall pay any price, bear any burden, meet any hardship, support any friend, oppose any foe to assure the survival and the success of liberty. *(Eisenhower glowers. Nixon looks shell-shocked. Then martial music and everyone scatters except Nixon and Washington)*

WASHINGTON   Nixon went back to California. He took a job in a law firm. He prepared to run for Governor in 1962. Meanwhile the new President launched an invasion of Cuba. *(Photographs of Bay of Pigs, Castro, confusion)* The invasion was a failure. The frightened President called in his various rivals and asked for their advice. *(Kennedy darts into view. Nixon pulls himself together for the new crisis)*

KENNEDY   What would *you* do now? About Cuba?

NIXON *(Sternly)*   I would find a proper legal cover—and go in. *(Shaking his head, Kennedy goes off. Nixon is now campaigning again but he is lackluster. Shakes hands)* I am running for Governor of the United States . . . I mean

(58)

California . . . *(Groups form. Pat beams at him. Pointing his finger straight at her, he declaims . . .)* California cannot afford to stand pat . . .

WASHINGTON   First he had to beat something called Goody Knight in the primary. *(While Nixon is wandering about, Kennedy and friend enter. They stand at attention. "Hail to the Chief" is played. On the screen, the Air Force in review)*

FRIEND   What does it feel like to be President?

KENNEDY   Well, it's a lot better than fucking around with Goody Knight in California. *(They exit. "The American People" are rolled into view)*

WASHINGTON   There was some talk of making the mysterious Howard Hughes loan to Nixon's brother an issue but . . .

NIXON *(Grimly)*   I'll dump a load of political bricks on anyone who tries to use it.

INTERVIEWER   Isn't it sort of embarrassing, having run for President to be running for just Governor?

NIXON   It takes an awful lot to embarrass me . . .

WASHINGTON   Six weeks after the Inaugural, Kennedy began a secret war in Southeast Asia. He committed American troops to shore up the regime of President Diem. Meanwhile, our hero won the Republican primary. He then faced Governor Pat Brown in the fall election.

NIXON   If elected I promise the best Communist control of any state. *(This doesn't have much effect on "The American People." Neither pedestal is in view, nor is Pat Brown. Nervously)* I advocate suspension of constitutional protection for certain persons, who under certain conditions, refuse to answer certain questions . . . What are our schools for, if not for indoctrination against Communism?

INTERVIEWER'S VOICE OVER   Governor Brown, why do you refuse to debate Mr. Nixon on television?

BROWN'S VOICE OVER   Because it would go by his rules. It'd be like going out to play baseball and finding out that someone brought a football instead. (*"The American People" head away from Nixon to Brown offstage*)

WASHINGTON   Our hero was defeated. (*Nixon stands center stage. Weeping, Pat disappears. Press gather like vultures. Nixon's press secretary approaches*)

SECRETARY   You should say something to the press.

NIXON   Screw them! Screw them! (*But, wild-eyed, Nixon approaches the press*)

Now that all the members of the press are so delighted that I have lost, I'd like to make a statement of my own. (*Electronic sounds bridge these sections . . . like a computer going wrong*)

Kennedy is all right if he can only get those who opposed atomic tests, who want him to admit Red China, all the woolly heads around—if he can just keep them away from him . . . (*More sounds*)

For sixteen years, ever since the Hiss case, you've had a lot of . . . a lot of fun—you've had an opportunity to attack me . . . (*Noises*)

The press have a right and responsibility, if they're against a candidate—to give him the shaft but also to recognize if they give him the shaft, put one lonely reporter on the campaign who will report what the candidate says now and then. (*More noises*)

As I leave, I want you to know—just think how much you'll be missing. You won't have Nixon to kick around any

more because, gentlemen, this is my last press conference. *(With that, Nixon is gone. Reporters are suitably
stunned)*

WASHINGTON *(To the audience)*   I think, at this point, we
all deserve a break.

Curtain

Phase Two

The curtain is up, as it was at the beginning of the first act. The chopped-down cherry tree is still upstage, as Washington appears, notes in hand.

WASHINGTON   It is the spring of 1963. Our hero kicks the dust of California from his shoes and moves to New York City. *(Nixon and Pat enter, carrying suitcases; the two doll-daughters roll along behind them. All stop center stage: their new home. On the screen flashes the name: "Mudge, Stern, Baldwin and Todd")*

Nixon joins a Wall Street law firm. *(The sign changes to "Nixon, Mudge, Rose, Guthrie, Alexander and Mitchell." Pat and the girls vanish. A desk appears. A chair. Nixon sits behind the desk. He smiles contentedly: a Wall Street lawyer at last)*

Nixon represents Pepsi-Cola. *(On screen flashes a huge Pepsi-Cola sign)*

Nixon also represents the children of the Dominican dictator Trujillo . . .

(65)

NIXON'S VOICE OVER   An illustrious ruler . . . *(On the screen a collage of Trujillo and family . . . of murders and general misbehavior in the Dominican Republic)*

WASHINGTON   . . . against their oldest brother Ramfis, who got off with most of their father's loot. Nixon went to Geneva to argue the case. He was not successful. *(During this, Nixon is becoming slightly restive. From a desk drawer he removes an elephant. Thoughtfully, he puts it in the center of his clean desk. A wistful moment. An interviewer appears)*

INTERVIEWER   Well, Mr. Nixon, in six months it will be 1964, another election year. Have you any plans to get into politics again? Run for governor of New York . . .

NIXON *(Firmly)*   I say categorically that I have no contemplation at all of being the candidate for anything in 1964, 1966, 1968 or 1972. Let's look at the facts. I have no staff. I am not answering my political mail. I am only making an occasional speech, writing an occasional magazine article. I have no political base. Anybody who thinks I could be a candidate for anything in any year is off his rocker. *(Nixon looks slightly off his rocker as he says this. The interviewer withdraws. To no one in particular)* I find when you get bored, you get tired. *(Nixon slumps)*

WASHINGTON   Meanwhile, back in Washington, President Kennedy continues his secret war in Vietnam. *(Kennedy and Generals enter. They hold an impromptu conference near Nixon's desk. He strains to overhear them. On the screen, a map of Vietnam)*

Shortly after his Inaugural in 1961, President Kennedy gave secret approval to "Operation Hades," later changed to "Operation Ranch Hand." *(On the screen we see planes engaged in defoliation)*

(66)

This operation involved the systematic defoliation of Vietnam. Jungles were destroyed, crops were destroyed. As a result, many civilians starved. But the Viet Cong continued to win. Finally, President Kennedy asked President Diem to request the presence of American troops in Vietnam. *(Diem flashes on screen)*

DIEM'S VOICE OVER   For American troops to come in would be not only a violation of the Geneva Accords but it would make me seem an American puppet.

WASHINGTON   In May 1961, Vice President Johnson was sent to Saigon to convince President Diem that he must ask for American troops.

JOHNSON'S VOICE OVER *(Booming)*   President Diem is the Winston Churchill of the Orient . . .

DIEM'S VOICE OVER *(Coldly)*   No.

WASHINGTON   But by October Diem had changed his mind. *(Kennedy and advisers look delighted)* Pretending to be a flood relief task force, American troops went into Vietnam. But this was not enough, according to General Maxwell Taylor, the President's favorite military adviser . . .

TAYLOR'S VOICE OVER   North Vietnam is extremely vulnerable to conventional bombing, a weakness which should be exploited diplomatically in convincing Hanoi to lay off South Vietnam.

WASHINGTON   President Kennedy's rationale for the secret war in Vietnam was to prevent the North with its Chinese and Russian allies from overrunning the South. But according to a secret government report . . .

(67)

OFFICIAL'S VOICE OVER   Throughout this time no one has ever found one Chinese rifle or one Soviet weapon used by a Viet Cong.

WASHINGTON   The weapons were homemade or captured from the South Vietnamese.

In 1963, President Diem, with the approval of the American government, was overthrown by a military junta. Unfortunately, President Diem and his brother were killed in the process . . . This was not, we are told, part of the game plan, as they say nowadays. *(On the screen, various shots of the coup. The murdered brothers. An interviewer approaches Kennedy and chiefs)*

INTERVIEWER   Mr. President, just what is the role of our advisers in Vietnam, and what is our policy toward the latest government?

KENNEDY   In the final analysis, it's their war. They're the ones who have to win it or lose it.

INTERVIEWER   In that case, why not bring home our soldiers?

KENNEDY *(Crisply)*   Withdrawal of United States troops would be a great mistake. *(Kennedy turns to his advisers)*

INTERVIEWER   Mr. President, just *what* are our objectives in Vietnam? *(Kennedy turns back to him, irritated)*

KENNEDY   We want the war to be won, the Communists to be contained, and our men to come home. We are not there to see a war lost. *(Nixon rises on this and gives Kennedy the OK sign. Interviewer, advisers go off)*

JOHNSON'S VOICE OVER   Mr. President, you have just got to come to Texas . . .

KENNEDY   Yes, Lyndon. *(A Southern Senator approaches)* Senator?

SENATOR   Mr. President, just what are your intentions in Vietnam. . . ?

KENNEDY   Well, I've ordered a study group to make . . . uh, recommendations . . .

SENATOR   From where I sit, you're getting yourself into a bigger and hotter war every day.

KENNEDY   After Cuba, Senator, I've got to go all the way with this one. *(Exeunt Kennedy and Senator)*

WASHINGTON   And so to Dallas. *(Three shots ring out. The sound of a dirge. The funeral procession on the screen, etc. Nixon comes downstage, very grave)*

NIXON   I was in a taxicab when I got the news. I had been in Dallas attending a meeting. I flew back to New York next morning. My cab stopped for a light in Queens and a guy ran over and said, Have you got a radio? The President's been wounded. I thought, Oh, my God, it must have been one of the nuts. *(Nixon turns to his desk, still talking)* A half-hour later I got to my apartment and the doorman told me he was dead. I called J. Edgar Hoover and asked him, What happened? Was it one of the nuts? Hoover said, No, it was a Communist. *(Nixon sits down, shaking his head. Unmasked, Kennedy enters and crosses downstage to Washington)*

KENNEDY   I must say, I never enjoy that part. But then, I never liked Dallas.

WASHINGTON   In my day it would've been unthinkable for an American to kill the First Magistrate . . .

KENNEDY   The world is different now . . .

WASHINGTON *(Grimly)*   Yes. And you made your contribution . . .

KENNEDY   I had no choice . . .

(69)

WASHINGTON *(Coldly)* We shall come to that presently. Now let us return to the living . . . *(Washington points to Nixon)*

KENNEDY Living? I think of Richard Nixon as sleeping at night in a box filled with earth from Transylvania . . . or maybe Pennsylvania, with its twenty-nine electoral votes. *(Nixon gives him a murderous look)*

WASHINGTON Lyndon Johnson is now the President. The New Frontier has become the Great Society. The social legislation President Kennedy was unable to get enacted has now become law under Johnson . . .

KENNEDY That is not correct. In my second term . . .

WASHINGTON There *was* no second term. You must content yourself with an invasion of Cuba that failed and a major war begun in Vietnam. That is quite enough for thirty-three months as President. *(Kennedy stalks offstage)*

Mr. Nixon is becoming interested in politics again. He makes an occasional statement. *(Nixon stares vaguely at the audience; he is still alone onstage, no one is listening)*

NIXON *(Warming up, awkwardly)* Red China and Russia are having their differences. They are simply arguing about what kind of shovel they should use to dig the grave of the United States. *(No response. Nixon looks discouraged. On the screen: various Johnson triumphs, Lady Bird, et al.)*

WASHINGTON Johnson is triumphant. Those Republicans who have said for thirty years that their candidates are simply faint echoes of the Democratic candidates now gather in the summer of 1964 at the Cow Palace in San Francisco. They want a real choice this time. They want Senator Barry Goldwater of

Arizona. *(On the screen: the Cow Palace. Convention non-sense. Nixon stares up at the screen, very sad. Then he turns to the audience; speaks firmly)*

NIXON   Looking to the future, it would be a tragedy for the Republican Party in the event that Senator Goldwater's views, as previously stated, were not challenged and repudiated. *(A chorus of boos. Nixon shrinks. Interviewer approaches)*

INTERVIEWER   How do you feel about the members of the press since your "last" press conference?

NIXON   My friends in the press—if I have any. If I haven't any maybe it was more my fault than theirs. I hope a man can lose his temper once in sixteen years and be forgiven for it.

INTERVIEWER'S VOICE OVER   Senator Goldwater, how would you characterize Mr. Nixon's presidential campaign four years ago?

GOLDWATER'S VOICE OVER   Hell, Nixon just went sashayin' around the country like shit through a cane-brake . . .

INTERVIEWER'S VOICE OVER   Mr. Nixon disagrees with some of your views . . .

GOLDWATER'S VOICE OVER   I guess he doesn't know my views very well. I got most of them from him. *(Nixon winces. An interviewer enters. He is plainly bored with the eager Nixon)*

INTERVIEWER   How do you explain Senator Goldwater's popularity?

NIXON   He has struck a chord among all the frustrated people in the country, the people who don't like to see us spend billions on foreign aid, the people who don't want Negroes to move into their neighborhoods, people who don't like taxes and who believe there are too many liberals in government.

INTERVIEWER   Do you think the possible presidential candidacy of Governor Wallace of Alabama will hurt the Republicans?

NIXON   No. It will leave the Fascist vote where it belongs —in that wing of the Democratic Party. *(Goldwater appears to accept the nomination. Cheering. Nixon joins him. Introduces him)*

There are some who say they will sit it out or take a boat ride. I say let's grow up, Republicans, and go to work! *(Nixon joins an interviewer downstage. To the interviewer)* Senator Goldwater should not moderate his views for political expedience. He is now in the mainstream of Republican philosophy.

GOLDWATER'S VOICE OVER   Extremism in the defense of liberty is no vice. Moderation in the pursuit of justice is no virtue . . . *(Nixon frowns. Goldwater, waving, goes off)*

EISENHOWER'S VOICE OVER   He would seem to say that the end always justifies the means. The whole American system reputes that idea.

INTERVIEWER *(To Nixon)*   Do you agree with that statement of Senator Goldwater?

NIXON   It's . . . uh, childish.

INTERVIEWER *(Yawning)*   What about Vietnam?

NIXON   There is no substitute for victory in South Vietnam.

INTERVIEWER   Neutralism?

NIXON   Neutralism where the Communists are concerned is only surrender on the installment plan. *(Nixon likes this hard-hitting phrase—is crestfallen at the inter-*

viewer's indifference) We must make it clear that we intend to win.

INTERVIEWER Castro?

NIXON The United States must make a decision that Castro must go and then do what is necessary to bring him down.

INTERVIEWER Don't you agree that the Johnson administration has done a lot for black people, for civil rights?

NIXON I am completely opposed to this kind of political demagoguery. We reject the idea that the way to reduce high Negro unemployment is to increase white unemployment.

INTERVIEWER What do you think of the Democratic Vice Presidential candidate, Hubert Humphrey?

NIXON *(Loftily)* I have never engaged in personalities in campaigns. *(The interviewer walks offstage, in bored disgust. Nixon addresses the audience)*

Let's be fair about it. Hubert Humphrey is a loyal American. But he is a dedicated radical. *(When there is no reply to this, Nixon slinks offstage. "The American People" are now rolled onto the stage. The usual bustle of an election. Goldwater and Johnson mount the pedestals. Johnson's mask beams benignly. Goldwater's mask looks puzzled)*

GOLDWATER Well, I'd drop a low-yield atomic bomb on the Chinese supply lines in North Vietnam. *(Everyone responds with horror, including Johnson, who mimes horror and outrage—vigorous head-shaking)*

WASHINGTON Senator Goldwater was of course simply revealing one of the administration's contingency plans.

GOLDWATER We are not just down there as advisers, we are down there with our boys and the boys are get-

ting shot. *(Johnson throws up his hands at this absurdity)*
Defoliation of the forests by low-yield atomic weapons
could well be done.

JOHNSON   Defoliation! Oh, no! *(General horror. Slyly Johnson taps his head: nuts. Winks at "The American People," who
are now practically crawling up into his lap)*

WASHINGTON   Senator Goldwater was only proposing
what the American Army had been doing in secret for
three years. *(Nixon appears. Addresses "The American People")*

NIXON   If Southeast Asia is allowed to fall, it will trigger
a big war to save the Philippines. *(But no one is listening)*

JOHNSON *(Sweet reason)*   We seek the full and effective
restoration of the international agreements signed in Geneva in 1954, with respect to South Vietnam. *(Everyone
onstage cheers. Then freezes)*

WASHINGTON   Actually, the United States had been in
violation of the Geneva Accords from the day Eisenhower supported Diem in preventing national elections. Under Kennedy the Accords were again violated
by introducing American troops into the South. Now,
a month before the 1964 election, Johnson has made
up his mind to escalate the war. But since he is the
peace candidate, he says nothing: He is swept into
office. *(Everyone unfreezes. Goldwater vanishes as Johnson
receives the homage of the nation. Then he withdraws, "The
American People" under one arm. Nixon goes back to his desk:
sits; removes another elephant from the desk drawer; puts it on
the desk. Is very thoughtful)*

In 1965, the Republican party was a ruin. So Nixon
began, cautiously, to campaign. *(Nixon is on his feet,
going into his campaign routine, shaking hands; pointing*

fingers; smiling oddly) No one paid much attention. All eyes were upon President Johnson and his escalation of the war.

JOHNSON'S VOICE OVER   The United States would never undertake the sacrifices these efforts require if its help were not wanted and requested.

WASHINGTON   Vice President Humphrey also had an insight into the war.

HUMPHREY'S VOICE OVER   Only the Viet Cong has committed atrocities in Vietnam.

NIXON   The way *not* to get the Communists to the conference table is to talk now about our willingness to negotiate . . .

WASHINGTON   A professor at Rutgers—a state university—had said that he welcomed a Viet Cong victory. Nixon took the position that any American has a right to free speech unless his salary is paid by a state or federal government. Nixon thought the professor should be fired.

NIXON   Leadership requires that the Governor step in and put the security of the nation above the security of the individual. We must never forget that if the war in Vietnam is lost the right of free speech will be extinguished throughout the world.

WASHINGTON   In 1966, Nixon traveled 30,000 miles and spoke in eighty-two Congressional districts for Republican candidates. (*Nixon campaigning. Definitely in better spirits*)

NIXON   Now that we've come part of the way with LBJ, we want no part of the rest of the way.

WASHINGTON   But Nixon did not object to the full-scale war Johnson had launched.

NIXON   Now that we have hit the oil supplies, we should not be inhibited by the fiction that targets in the Hanoi areashouldnotbehit.*(Applausefromhawks)*

There is no reasonable possibility of a negotiated settlement . . . It simply encourages the enemy that we are begging for peace. *(More campaigning)*

The war on poverty has been first in promises, first in politics, first in press releases, and last in performance. *(The press gather about him)*

I oppose those well-intentioned but mistaken Democrats who want to retreat to coastal enclaves in South Vietnam and indefinitely suspend air attacks against the North.

INTERVIEWER   Do you still want to be President?

NIXON   Just the chance of being President isn't enough. It's the battle that counts.

WASHINGTON   In November, just before the election, Nixon attacked President Johnson for not doing enough in Vietnam. It was a slack afternoon at *The New York Times*, so they put the Nixon story on page one . . . *(On screen, front page with Nixon's attack. Nixon looks up, sees front page, does a little dance of joy)* Nixon was back in circulation.

INTERVIEWER'S VOICE OVER   Mr. President, what did you think of Mr. Nixon's recent attack on you in the *Times . . .?*

JOHNSON'S VOICE OVER   He never did really recognize what was going on when he had an official position in the government. . . . He doesn't serve his country well, this chronic campaigner—in the hope he can pick up a precinct or two or a ward or two. *(Nixon is ecstatic. Jumps up and down)*

(76)

WASHINGTON   The Republicans made a great come-back in the congressional elections.

NIXON   There was a big swing vote in the last days. Johnson's attack made it swing our way . . .

WASHINGTON   Nixon was given full credit for the victory.

NIXON   We'll kick their toes off in 1968! *(A couch, Dr. Hutschnecker, and a chair are rolled into view)*

WASHINGTON   During this period it is alleged that Nixon went to a psychotherapist named Dr. Hutschnecker. *(Nixon lies down on the couch)* When the story later broke in the press, Nixon's office said that Dr. Hutschnecker had treated him for a physical ailment. *(Nixon weeps softly. Hutschnecker nods sympathetically. Then Nixon rises, with an uneasy glance at the audience. Couch, chair and shrink vanish)*

WASHINGTON   During 1967, opposition to the Vietnam war was building. There was also violence in the cities. Black against white. Riots. Fires. Newark burns. *(A montage of riots, burning ghettos. Nixon addresses the audience)*

NIXON   I have great concern about the next summer unless the peace forces—the police, national guard—will be ready and deal without fear or favor with any kind of lawlessness. *(Reporters begin to gather about him)*

I believe the Republican nominee, whoever he is, can beat Johnson and if I am the Republican nominee, I can beat Johnson. That is a self-serving statement and so intended. *(A decrepit Eisenhower appears, carrying a golf club. Lines up a shot)*

INTERVIEWER   General, what about Vietnam?

(77)

EISENHOWER *(Mechanically)* Whatever happens in Vietnam, I can conceive of nothing except military victory.

INTERVIEWER What is your view of the new Nixon?

EISENHOWER He's really matured. *(Eisenhower goes off. Nixon puts on a helmet liner. Marches about the stage)*

WASHINGTON Nixon made a quick trip to Saigon. After a meeting with Ambassador Lodge, he said . . .

NIXON We had a very interesting discussion and, actually, we made a deal. He is going to put a Pepsi-Cola cooler in the Embassy in Saigon. *(Nixon removes the helmet liner. At large)* No politician is dead until he admits it.

INTERVIEWER Mr. Nixon, what about your image?

NIXON *(Sadly)* They still call me Tricky Dick. It's a brutal thing to fight. If anyone takes the time to check my public record fairly—and it's all there—the votes I cast, the speeches I made, the things I wrote, he'd have to conclude that on the great issues of the past twenty years my record is clear and consistent.

INTERVIEWER Do you believe that China should be admitted to the United Nations?

NIXON We simply cannot afford to leave China forever outside the family of nations, there to nurture its fantasies, cherish its hates and threaten its neighbors. *(Slight shock amongreporters. Nixonhasnotednoinconsistency)*

INTERVIEWER Tell us, who are your friends?

NIXON In my job you can't enjoy the luxury of intimate personal friendships. You can't confide absolutely in anyone.

INTERVIEWER It has been alleged that recently on *The Jack Paar Show* you actually made little jokes about yourself? Is this allegation true?

NIXON *(Twitch of a smile)* This is a generation that wants to laugh, a generation that wants to be entertained. I guess television made it that way.

INTERVIEWER Was it a good idea to go to war in Vietnam?

NIXON The decision to go to war was right and history will so regard it.

INTERVIEWER More and more people think it was wrong . . .

NIXON I will not shift my position because of a shift in public sentiment . . . If you're asking me if I intend to accommodate my views just to woo the liberals, the answer is, hell no!

INTERVIEWER Your image . . .

NIXON I'm not going to take any speech lessons. I'm not hiring any high-powered public relations firms. When a man is constrained or artificial, he doesn't get through.

INTERVIEWER Do you think that you get through to intelligent people?

NIXON Some people say I oversimplify. Well, that's the way I am. I ask questions to wake up the guy in the audience. It's the Socratic approach. I didn't invent it. But it drives the intellectuals nuts.

INTERVIEWER The press . . .

NIXON The establishment press underestimates me . . . I really do have convictions. For example, Vietnam—and I'm not going to change those convictions for political reasons . . .

INTERVIEWER You are considered, by some, to be emotionally unstable . . .

NIXON Okay, I blew up in 1962. I was tired, worn out, sick at heart. The press sniping all through the campaign had been fierce. So I blew up. I regretted it later, but I'll say this, it cleared the air . . .

INTERVIEWER   But suppose, as President, you get tired, worn out, sick at heart, with the press sniping at you, and there is an international crisis, will you blow up? *(Nixon has got away from this questioner, smiling nervously)*

WASHINGTON   Nixon is now ready for the prize he has sought all his life. *(Kennedy enters)*

KENNEDY   I have to watch this part. *(Nixon meets a group of pols and press. TV in evidence. Moment of destiny)*

WASHINGTON   In the cold early spring of 1968, he entered the primaries in New Hampshire.

NIXON   Ladies and gentlemen, as we start this campaign there's one thing we should say at the outset—this is *not* my last press conference. *(Dutiful laughter)*

WASHINGTON   Nixon won in New Hampshire. But most of the country was more interested in the successful campaign of Senator Eugene McCarthy to replace President Johnson. *(Shots of McCarthy and the young in New Hampshire)*

NIXON   Never in the history of this country have we been in more trouble in more places in the world than we are today.

WASHINGTON   Nixon goes into other primaries.

NIXON   This country cannot tolerate a long war. The Asians have no respect for human lives. They don't care about body counts.

WASHINGTON   Nixon heats up the campaign.

NIXON   I'm not going to sit here in a presidential campaign and say that Lyndon Johnson is lying to the American people about Vietnam . . . *(Eyes dart about: Is it working again?*) He is a patriotic American, *but* he has shown a lack of understanding.

JOHNSON'S VOICE OVER   Shit!

NIXON   I wouldn't charge Lyndon Johnson with lying, just a failure to communicate . . . The country hasn't won a hand since he started to deal.

WASHINGTON   In April 1968 President Johnson addressed the nation.

JOHNSON'S VOICE OVER   I have concluded that I should not permit the Presidency to become involved in the partisan divisions that are developing in this political year. Accordingly, I shall not seek and I will not accept the nomination of my party for another term as President . . .

KENNEDY   I would never have done that.

WASHINGTON   President Johnson felt he couldn't win the war or make peace . . .

JOHNSON'S VOICE OVER   I feel like a houndbitch in heat in the country. If you run, they chew your tail off. If you stand still, they slip it to you.

KENNEDY   Very colorful. Very descriptive.

JOHNSON'S VOICE OVER   Every time I stop the bombing of North Vietnam, they run those trucks of theirs up my ass.

KENNEDY   A very tempting thing to do.

JOHNSON'S VOICE OVER   I got earphones in Moscow and Manila, earphones in Rangoon, and earphones in Hanoi and all I hear on them is "Fuck you, Lyndon Johnson."

KENNEDY   Much my own sentiment.

WASHINGTON   Nixon attempts to inspire.

KENNEDY   I'm all ears.

NIXON   This country must move again—how long will it take the United States to move?

KENNEDY   Plagiarist. *(To Washington)* You know, in 1960, every time I said let's get America moving again, the next day I'd go *down* in the polls. It sounded as if I wanted every one to get up at five o'clock.

WASHINGTON   The Nixon of the primaries was a human Nixon, full of insights into his own character . . .

NIXON   I eat cottage cheese until it runs out of my ears . . . I put catsup on it . . . catsup disguises almost anything . . . *(Clears his throat: new insight)* I believe in hitting back when someone attacks, my instinct is to strike back.

WASHINGTON   Nixon appeared on the popular television program *Laugh-in.*

NIXON   *(Very showbiz)*   Sock it to me! Sock it to me! Sock it to me!

KENNEDY   There are some things you don't do even to be President.

NIXON   *(Hears this, a sneer)*   Like what?

WASHINGTON   Now, gentlemen, you're breaking the frame.

NIXON   *(Piously)*   The three passions of Quakers are peace, civil rights and tolerance. That's why, as a Quaker I can't be an extremist, a racist or an uncompromising hawk.

WASHINGTON   *(Startled)*   What?

NIXON   While all this may seem to be the opposite of what I've stood for, I'm actually consistent.

KENNEDY   The old Nixon. *(Mimics)* Actually, I'm for winning the war while getting out. Luckily, people have no memory.

NIXON   *(Nods)*   Voters quickly forget what a man says.

KENNEDY   That's from his book *Six Crises*. Note how I say "his book" because no one remembers there was such a book. Why, they've even forgotten the first act.

INTERVIEWER   Why do you think you're doing so well in the polls?

NIXON   In times of trouble people want reassurance, a man they know and can rely on—just as the French sought out De Gaulle in France . . .

KENNEDY   Megalomania.

INTERVIEWER   What do you plan to do for the black minority?

NIXON   I have serious doubts that anything I say will get a majority of the Negro vote.

KENNEDY   He also doesn't need them. All the blacks and all of those under twenty-five together make up just one-fourth of the electorate. If you run *against* that one-fourth you will be very popular with the average voter who is white and forty-seven and worried.

NIXON   For most of us in America the American Revolution has been won and the American dream achieved.

KENNEDY   See?

INTERVIEWER   You seem to favor recognition of Red China.

NIXON   I think it possible to reach the point where recognition can be discussed but not now.

INTERVIEWER   Off the record, how do you view the Presidency?

NIXON   I've always thought the country could run itself domestically without a President. All you need is a competent Cabinet to run the country at home. You need a President for foreign policy. No Secretary of State is really important. The President makes foreign policy.

(83)

KENNEDY   He'll be sorry.

WASHINGTON   The real action that spring and summer was in the Democratic Party. *(Nixon goes offstage. The screen now dominates the stage)* Senator McCarthy defeated Lyndon Johnson. Now Senator Robert Kennedy, the heir apparent to Camelot, sets out to defeat McCarthy . . .

KENNEDY   Camelot! You don't know how I hate that word. It was Jackie, of course. Imagine using the title of a musical comedy to describe my administration . . . a *flop* musical comedy . . .

WASHINGTON   Worse things will be said of your administration, Mr. President. *(A shot rings out)* Martin Luther King was shot. *(Scenes of his death and funeral)*

WASHINGTON   In Oregon, McCarthy defeated Kennedy.

KENNEDY   Strange state, Oregon.

WASHINGTON   The final contest took place in California . . . *(Shots of campaigning. McCarthy. Bobby Kennedy)*

BOBBY'S VOICE OVER   Senator McCarthy, you say you are going to take ten thousand black people and move them into Orange County . . .

MCCARTHY'S VOICE OVER   I did not say that. What I said was . . . *(A pistol shot)*

WASHINGTON   Senator Kennedy is murdered, too. *(Rounds on Kennedy)* What sort of country have you made? *(During this, on the screen, funeral train—crowds—ominous mood building)*

KENNEDY   We didn't make it. But we tried to make it better.

WASHINGTON   In what way?

KENNEDY   We found it insupportable that blacks should be discriminated against, that twenty-five million people should exist at the poverty level . . .

WASHINGTON   So you *found* it but what did you *do?*

KENNEDY   In the short time that was granted us . . .

WASHINGTON   You did nothing, either of you, but play to the passions of the mob.

KENNEDY   That is not true . . .

WASHINGTON   In thirty-three months what did you do for the poor, for the black . . . ?

KENNEDY   We could get nothing through Congress because . . .

WASHINGTON   Johnson got his program through in three months.

KENNEDY   First, there was Cuba, then there was Vietnam . . .

WASHINGTON   Yes, you tried to invade the one, and you began a secret war in the other, in direct violation of the spirit of that Constitution you swore—as did I—to uphold . . .

KENNEDY   The world is not as simple now as it was in 1799.

WASHINGTON   Right action is simple. I put the case that you were entirely governed by self-love, by expediency, by a desire to be first in the nation without the slightest responsibility to the people who believed your rhetoric.

KENNEDY *(Cold fury)*   I put the case that great empires are complex matters beyond the understanding of that agrarian colony whose first President you were.

WASHINGTON   And in that word "empire," Mr. President, you betray yourself, the people and the Constitution, for no democracy, no republic, can survive once it aspires to dominion over other people in other lands against their will.

KENNEDY   I could not have changed the thrust of our history, even had I wanted to. *(A pause)*

WASHINGTON *(Looks at his paper)*   By summer, Nixon has all but wrapped up the Republican nomination. His chief rivals are Rockefeller and Reagan. Reagan is the heir of Goldwater. The delegates love him. But Nixon has their votes. *(Nixon appears with press, pols, TV, the doll-daughters, accompanied by a Howdy Doody doll labeled "David." A triumphant mood)*

Incidentally, Nixon's financing came not only from the oil interests but from mutual funds. Until recently, Nixon was a director in four mutual funds of the Investors Diversified Services group, which includes Investors Mutual. With assets of 2.8 billion dollars, this is the largest mutual fund in the world.

KENNEDY   General, the public has no interest in these matters.

WASHINGTON *(Ignores him)* Before the convention, Nixon wrote a secret letter to a number of brokers promising to lay off, if elected.

NIXON'S VOICE OVER   The Johnson administration has further sought wide-sweeping new regulatory powers over the mutual fund industry, which powers would be tantamount to rate-fixing in a highly competitive industry. The Johnson administration believes the government can make decisions for the investor better than he can make them for himself. This philosophy I reject.

WASHINGTON   On the day before the nomination Nixon held a closed meeting with the Southern delegates. Unknown to him his remarks were tape-recorded.

DELEGATE   What about open housing?

NIXON   Conditions are different in different parts of the country—just like gun control—and ought to be handled at the state level rather than the federal level . . . In my view —and I think it vitally important to get the civil rights and open-housing issues out of sight so we didn't have a split party over the platform when we came down here to Miami Beach.

WASHINGTON   Nixon also committed himself to winning the war in Vietnam. When a recording of this conversation was released, an embarrassed aide said . . .

AIDE'S VOICE OVER   Nixon said some of these things but not all. Maybe a few words here or there were not distinguishable—things may have sounded mumbled.

WASHINGTON   Nixon was nominated. *(Nixon is now center stage. Pat beams. Dolls are lined up beside him. Festive mood)*

NIXON   This time we're going to win! *(Cheers are heard)* General Eisenhower, as you know, lies critically ill in the Walter Reed Hospital tonight. I have talked, however, with Mrs. Eisenhower on the telephone. She tells me there is nothing he lives more for, and there is nothing that would lift him more than to win in November. And I say let's win this one for Ike! *(Roar of applause, Nixon raises arms: victory signal waggles)*

WASHINGTON   In gratitude to the Southern states which had made his nomination possible, Nixon chose as his running mate the first-term Governor of Maryland, Spiro Agnew . . .

(87)

NIXON *(Intones)* "A man of compassion." *(A chorus of "Who?" A grim-faced Agnew, masked, appears. Solemnly)* There can be a mystique about a man. You can look him in the eye and know he's got it. He's got a lot to say.

WASHINGTON   With Robert Kennedy dead, the Democratic contest was now between Vice President Humphrey and Senator McCarthy. Their forces met in Chicago, at the bloodiest convention in national history. *(Shots of police beating up everyone in sight)* In the course of a police riot, Humphrey was nominated, and the party was hopelessly split. *(Now the pedestals and "The American People" appear. Nixon mounts his pedestal. Humphrey mounts his. Agnew takes up his position below Nixon. Ranged nearby are Pat and the dolls)*

Nixon's strategy was to avoid as much as possible the issues. He turned his campaign over to a New York advertising agency. They kept him on television in a controlled format. This time the product was going to be packaged properly. Nixon refused to debate Humphrey.

HUMPHREY   Mr. Nixon is having his own debate. I have a feeling the new Nixon and the old Nixon are going to go at it for some time, and we're going to see the *real* Nixon, and you're not going to like it.

NIXON *(Smiles benignly)*   If you want your President to continue the do-nothing policy toward crime, vote for Humphrey.

HUMPHREY   Mr. Nixon is a compulsive cold warrior.

AGNEW *(Suddenly)*   Humphrey mistakes firmness for inflexibility. Humphrey is squishy soft. Humphrey has been soft on inflation, soft on Communism, and soft on law and order over the years. *(Nixon smiles on "soft on Com-*

munism." During this "The American People" just jiggle, not for one or the other)

VOICE OVER   Is Hubert Humphrey really a Communist? *(Agnew starts to answer in the affirmative when Nixon picks up a butterfly net on a long pole and places it over Agnew's head)*

NIXON   I and Agnew will question the policies but *not* the loyalty of the Democratic candidates. *(Butterfly net is removed)*

AGNEW   *(Contritely)*   If I left the impression that the Vice President is not a loyal American, I want to rectify that. I said "squishy soft" and I'm not proud of it.

KENNEDY   There *is* a new Nixon. And his name is Agnew.

NIXON   I picked Spiro Agnew and I think he's a good pick.

AGNEW   When I look out at a crowd, I don't see there a Negro, there an Italian, there a Polack . . . *(The butterfly net comes down again)*

NIXON   In a Nixon administration students will have a better alternative than to take to the streets to protest. They are going to have a piece of the action. *(Nixon removes butterfly net)*

AGNEW   Once you've seen one slum, you've seen them all. *(The net goes down again)*

NIXON   The real answer to progress in America is not to wait for the *government* to do something but to wait for the *people* to do something. *(Butterfly net comes off Agnew)*

AGNEW   You may give us your symptoms. We will make the diagnosis and we, the establishment, will implement the cure. *(A woman reporter approaches Mrs. Nixon)*

WASHINGTON   The journalist Gloria Steinem was able to get Mrs. Nixon—for the first time—to talk about herself, her dreams, her ideals . . .

STEINEM   What woman in history would you most like to be?

PAT   Mrs. Eisenhower . . .

STEINEM   Why?

PAT   Because she meant so much to young people.

STEINEM   I was in college when she was in the White House and I don't think she meant much of anything to the young.

PAT *(Grimly)*   Well, I do. *(Pause. Nixon strains to hear)* I never had time to think about things like that, who I wanted to be, or who I admired, or to have ideas. I never had time to dream about anyone else. I had to work. My parents died when I was a teenager, and I had to work my way through college. I drove people all the way across the country so I could get to New York and take training as an X-ray technician so I could work my way through college. I worked in a bank while Dick was in the service. Oh, I could have sat for those months doing nothing like everybody else, but I worked in the bank and talked with people and learned about all their funny little customs . . . I don't have time to worry about who I admire or who I identify with. I've never had it easy. I'm not like all you . . . *(During these last sentences, Nixon has picked up the butterfly net and it is hovering over Pat's head. He is definitely alarmed but Pat is herself now)* . . . all those people who had it easy. *(Brightly, perkily)* Now, I hope we see you again soon. I really do. Bye, now. Take care. *(Steinem goes. Pat rejoins the dolls)*

KENNEDY   And they wondered why I never let Jackie open her mouth in public.

REPORTER   Are you going to sell TVA if you're President?

NIXON *(Gravely)*   No, no, I have no plans to sell it.

(90)

WASHINGTON   Nixon spent most of his time on television. Answering questions that had been planted for him by his aides. He spent twenty-two and a half million dollars on television. *(Nixon steps off the pedestal. Addresses a group of TV technicians)*

NIXON   We're going to build this whole campaign around television. You fellows just tell me what you want me to do and I'll do it. *(They pounce on him, paint him, guide him about, as cameras turn: he is more than ever the mechanical man)* I sweat too much. *("The American People" are still jiggling)*

AIDE'S VOICE OVER   For the Philadelphia show we've got this psychiatrist to ask him . . .

ANOTHER AIDE'S VOICE OVER   Jesus Christ! Don't you know Nixon hates psychiatrists? Get rid of him!

NIXON   I say that after four years of war in Asia, after 25,000 dead, 200,000 casualties, America needs new leadership. *(Nixon mounts the pedestal)*

HUMPHREY   If you know how to end the war and bring peace to the Pacific, Mr. Candidate, let the American people hear your formula now. Why wait until next year?

NIXON   No one with this responsibility who is seeking office should give away any of his bargaining position in advance. Under no circumstances should a man say what he would do next January.

KENNEDY   Of course he had no plan. He still has no plan. But the people fell for it.

WASHINGTON   In St. Petersburg, Florida, a policeman accompanying Nixon's motorcade fell off his motorcycle, breaking his arm, his ankle, and opening a bleeding head wound. *(A policeman does a tumble downstage. Nixon approaches him)*

(91)

NIXON I'm sorry. Are you all right?

POLICEMAN Yes, sir. I'm only sorry about delaying you, sir. *(Nixon and policeman stare at each other for a long moment while Nixon tries to think of something to say)*

NIXON Do you like the work? *(Policeman vanishes. Agnew is now being heckled by the young)*

AGNEW You can renounce your citizenship if you don't like it here. *(Nixon grabs the butterfly net)* So why don't you leave? *(To the audience)* When we're elected, they're going to dry up and disappear from this country very quickly.

NIXON *(Suddenly)* I have traveled far in this campaign: Indianapolis, Concord, Atlanta, Santa Monica, Dallas, Akron, Lansing, Charlotte, Houston, Chattanooga, Spartanburg, Kansas City, Johnstown, Pa., Greensboro, Springfield, Burbank, Toledo, Minneapolis, Phoenix, Buffalo, Denver, San Francisco, Flint . . . *(The names are ticked off compulsively. An end in themselves)*

WASHINGTON On November fifth, 1968, 73,186,819 voted. In a close election Richard Nixon was elected President. Yet only one in four of those qualified to vote actually chose Nixon. *(During this, Humphrey et al. vanish. Nixon is left alone with Pat and the dolls. Nixon addresses the audience)*

NIXON *(Warmly)* In Deshler, Ohio, at the end of a long day of whistle-stopping . . . a teenager held up a sign "Bring Us Together." And that will be the great objective of this administration at the outset, to bring the American people together . . .

KENNEDY Yes. Bring them together. Then watch them fight.

NIXON *(Thoughtfully)* If I had my life to live over, I would have liked to have ended up as a sportswriter.

(92)

WASHINGTON   At the Inaugural Nixon was low-key. *(Nixon is center stage . . . scene same as at the Kennedy Inauguration)*

NIXON   America has suffered from a fever of words; from inflated rhetoric that promises more than it can deliver; from angry rhetoric that fans discontent into hatreds; from bombastic rhetoric that postures instead of persuading. We cannot learn from one another until we stop shouting at one another.

KENNEDY   He is incredible. But then so are the American people who forget what he's done, what he is.

NIXON   An era of confrontation has ended. An era of negotiation has begun. *(To a blast of trumpets, exeunt Nixon et al. Washington and Kennedy remain onstage)*

KENNEDY   Curiously uninspiring, didn't you think?

WASHINGTON   Yes. But at least his speech was not as aggressive as the one Mr. Sorenson wrote for your Inaugural.

KENNEDY   I admit that Sorenson's speeches were not in the same class as the ones that Alexander Hamilton used to write for you but . . . *(Eisenhower enters)*

EISENHOWER   Well, here I am. Dead at last. Those goddam doctors keep you around just as long as you're able to breathe and pay their bills. Kennedy, I'd forgotten all about that Dallas thing when I first saw you tonight. One thing I'd like to ask, were you satisfied with that report—you know, the one that what's-his-name put out. You know, the big fellow, California, white hair . . .

KENNEDY   Earl Warren.

EISENHOWER   Yeah. Worse damn mistake I ever made putting him on the Court. Were you satisfied with the findings that only that one fellow, what's-his-name, Osbert? shot you?

KENNEDY I'm hardly the person to ask. It was very quick. But I will have a few questions for Mr. Castro when he gets here. And the CIA. And Lyndon.

WASHINGTON You must admit there was a kind of justice in your being killed.

KENNEDY *(Flatly)* Oh? Thank you.

EISENHOWER *(Nods)* Mmm. I know what you mean, General, but . . .uh, I think, well, that's going a little far. I know it *could* happen to any of us . . .

WASHINGTON But it is more apt to happen to the leader of a predatory empire which is trying, through force, to conquer the world . . .

EISENHOWER Now . . . now, I think that is an . . . uh, exaggerated view of the American presence abroad . . . uh, militarily and . . .

KENNEDY *(Coolly)* It is not exaggerated. *(To Washington)* But what is wrong with conquering the world?

WASHINGTON You tell me. You were murdered, your brother was murdered, more citizens are murdered in the streets of the United States than in all the other Western countries put together. And of course your armies specialize in murdering civilians by the million . . .

KENNEDY But that is the way things are. The way they've always been.

EISENHOWER Well, up to a point . . .

KENNEDY The United States has six percent of the world's population. Yet Americans use forty percent of the world's raw resources. That is why we are in Vietnam.

EISENHOWER   Well, you never said anything like that
while you were alive . . . at least no one ever told me
you did. I don't read the papers, you know . . .

KENNEDY   There has been time for reflection.

WASHINGTON   Then have you had time to reflect why
the United States should have set itself upon the kind
of course that those of us who founded the Republic
swore was contrary to the deepest interest of a unique
people engaged in a unique political experiment?

KENNEDY   The experiment was unique as long as
there was an empty continent to fill. Well, General, we
filled it. We broke every treaty we made with the Indi-
ans, we stole their land, we slaughtered them. By 1900
we had no place to go. There was an economic depres-
sion. So we began a war with Spain, deliberately pro-
voked by us, and we won, and that gave us the
Philippines, where we killed a great many people and
established ourselves as a power in the Pacific. Ever
since we have been on the march. From the Philippines to Japan, from Japan to the mainland of Asia, to
Korea, to Indo-China . . .

EISENHOWER   I remember when I went ashore at Nor-
mandy, around me the greatest fleet the world had
ever seen, and overhead an armada such as Leonardo
da Vinci never dreamed of, and there in front of me
was the Old World where we came from—on its knees,
but glad to see us, glad we were there, as liberators
. . . naturally . . .

WASHINGTON   You are both . . . insupportable.

KENNEDY   And you, General, are either blind or a fool.

WASHINGTON   You have made the United States the
sort of country from which your ancestors fled. To us

it was unthinkable that Americans would draft men into the army in peacetime. It was unthinkable that Presidents conduct secret wars. It was unthinkable . . .

KENNEDY   We are no different from any other power that has had its moment. That is the truth about ourselves, and the sooner we learn it, the wiser we will be.

WASHINGTON   Certainly, the more cynical, the more knowing . . .

EISENHOWER *(Indicates Kennedy)*   Well, what he says is *half* true. Naturally, I tried to keep the peace. I advised against any harebrained land war on the mainland of Asia . . .

KENNEDY *(Astonished)*   Did you, now? Well, let's hear again what you said to me the week before my Inauguration.

EISENHOWER'S VOICE OVER   It is imperative that Laos be defended. The United States should accept this task with our allies, if we could persuade them, and alone if we could not. Our unilateral intervention would be our last desperate hope in the event we were unable to prevail upon the other signatories to join us.

EISENHOWER   Well . . . uh, naturally, I expected our . . . uh, allies to . . .

KENNEDY   And, God knows, that fuck-up in Cuba was the result of *your* planning . . .

EISENHOWER   Look, sonny, what I *might've* done is not the point, what I did *not* do is history. I kept the peace.

WASHINGTON   Are you gentlemen satisfied with what you did?

EISENHOWER   All in all, yes . . .

KENNEDY   I'll pass on that question.

WASHINGTON   Now the Nixon administration begins.

KENNEDY *(Softly)*   Jesus.

EISENHOWER   If you don't mind, I'll just practice my putting. I can . . . uh, imagine what Dick will be like as President . . . *(Eisenhower putts his way across stage— and off—as Nixon, very presidential, appears with press and TV. He mimes foreign travel, crowds)*

WASHINGTON   Shortly after the election Nixon made a brief ceremonial trip to Europe. The only memorable thing he said . . .

NIXON'S VOICE OVER   In the sense that the people of Berlin stand for freedom and peace, all the people of the world are truly Berliners.

WASHINGTON   Then he came home, where everyone was interested to know just how he would end the war in Vietnam.

INTERVIEWER   Do you consider it possible to have a cease-fire in Vietnam as long as Viet Cong still occupy Vietnamese territory?

NIXON   Cease-fire is a term of art that really has no relevance in my opinion to guerrilla war. I think at this point that this administration believes that the better approach is mutual withdrawal of forces as a guaranteed basis by both sides from South Vietnam.

INTERVIEWER   Any plans for improving relations with China?

NIXON   The policy of this country and the administration, at this time, will be to continue to *oppose* Communist China's admission to the UN.

INTERVIEWER   You spoke a great deal about the need for law and order during your campaign. What do you plan to do about law and order right here in Washington, where

(97)

people are murdered, robbed and raped within sight of the White House?

NIXON   My advisers tell me that by seeing that the area is better lighted that perhaps the possibility of purse snatching and other crimes in the vicinity of the White House might be reduced—therefore we have turned on the lights in all that area, I can assure you . . .

INTERVIEWER   What about the poor?

NIXON   I do not see a reasonable prospect that I will recommend . . . a guaranteed annual income or a negative income tax.

INTERVIEWER   The economy?

NIXON   I do not go along with the suggestion that inflation can be effectively controlled by exhorting labor and management and industry to follow certain guide-lines . . .

INTERVIEWER'S VOICE OVER   Mr. Agnew, how did you feelaboutthewaythepresstreatedyouinthecampaign?

AGNEW'S VOICE OVER   Six months ago, I was a fairly pop-ular and successful Governor. Now I'm being called the village idiot. (*On the screen, shots of fighting in Vietnam*)

WASHINGTON   The war continued. In March Nixon said . . .

NIXON   There is no prospect for a reduction of American forces in the foreseeable future.

WASHINGTON   Nixon also proposed a costly system of nuclear ABM's to defend the United States . . .

NIXON   It is a safeguard against any attack by the Chi-nese Communists that we can foresee over the next ten years.

WASHINGTON   In April 1969 Nixon said . . . (*On screen appear statistics: to date, 33,641 Americans dead, etc.*)

NIXON   We have no plans to reduce our troops until there is more progress. I will make this promise: next year I will be able to report that we have made real progress toward bringing peace in the world, reestablishing law and order, and also in stopping the rise in taxes and inflation. This is our goal. We are not over-promising.   .

WASHINGTON   In June 1969 Nixon said . . .

NIXON   I have decided to order the immediate deployment from Vietnam of 25,000 men.

WASHINGTON   Then on the fourth of June, the old Nixon reappeared. At the Air Force Academy, in Colorado. *(Nixon marches along, very much the commander-in-chief. On the screen ranks of cadets, flags, etc. Nixon's speech is broken with bars of martial music)*

NIXON   I should just like to give you one impression that shows you there is some continuity in history. Dwight David Eisenhower II, the grandson of General Eisenhower, and his namesake, as he saw this beautiful country and looked to the mountains off to the distance, said "Gee, this is great country." I want you to know that I agree ... *(Pause as though for applause which does not come. Instead a beat or two of "Wild Blue Yonder." He frowns)* It is open season on the armed forces. Military programs are ridiculed as needless, if not deliberate, waste. The military profession is derided in some of the so-called best circles in America. Patriotism is considered by some to be a backward fetish of the uneducated and unsophisticated. *(A rousing blare of trumpets)* I believe that every man in uniform is a citizen first and a serviceman second. *(More music)* In the past generation since 1941 this nation has paid for fourteen years of peace with fourteen years of war.

(99)

KENNEDY *(To Washington)* See? *(Nixon's mouth continues to move; but the sound is off)*

WASHINGTON It is my impression that the United States has been at war for the better part of the twentieth century.

KENNEDY As a result, we are the first in the world . . .

WASHINGTON But for how long?

NIXON The American war dead of this generation has been far greater than all of the preceding generations of American history. In terms of human suffering, this has been the costliest generation in the two centuries of our history.

WASHINGTON Enough. Enough. *(Nixon steps to one side, as Agnew enters. Young people with placards: "Out of Vietnam!" etc.)*

AGNEW In my judgment, the war in Vietnam would be over today if we could simply stop the demonstrations in the United States.

WASHINGTON While Nixon was speaking against "the so-called best circles" in the United States, the Vice President was hardening the same message.

AGNEW A society which comes to fear its children is effete. A sniveling hand-wringing power structure deserves the violent rebellion it encourages. If my generation doesn't stop cringing, yours will inherit a lawless society where emotion and muscle displace reason. *(Nixon smiles, nods his head)* As for these deserters, malcontents, radicals, incendiaries, the civil and uncivil disobedients among our young SDS, PLP, Weathermen I and Weathermen II, the Revolutionary Action Movement, the Yippies, the hippies, yahoos, black panthers, lions and tigers alike—I

(100)

would swap the whole damn zoo for a single platoon of the kind of young Americans I saw in Vietnam. (*Cheering on screen. Nixon applauds loudly, vigorously*)

NIXON'S VOICE OVER   We cannot learn from one another until we stop shouting at one another. (*Nixon ignores this line from his own Inaugural*)

WASHINGTON   Pressures mount for Nixon to end the war. (*A press conference forms about Nixon*)

INTERVIEWER   Former defense secretary Clark Clifford has suggested that a hundred thousand troops ought to be out by the end of the year, and all ground troops out by the end of '70. Is that a realistic timetable?

NIXON (*Irritated*)   As far as how many will be withdrawn —I would hope that we could beat Mr. Clifford's timetable, just as I think we've done a little better than he did when he was in charge of our national defense.

WASHINGTON   In July the commander-in-chief visited Vietnam. (*Nixon puts on a military hat. Approaches a row of troops. One of them is black. Nixon speaks to various soldiers*)

NIXON   And where are you from?

SOLDIER   Texas.

NIXON   Texas! I'll be darned. Think the Cowboys can beat the Packers this year?

SOLDIER   I hope so, sir.

NIXON   They've lost their quarterback, you know. And where are you from?

SOLDIER   Chicago.

NIXON   Chicago! Have you seen the Cubs this year? They might take it all. Are you a Cub or White Sox fan?

SOLDIER   I'm a Yankee fan, sir. (*Nixon stares unhappily at the black soldier. Neither can think of anything to say*)

(101)

NIXON   Do they ever get any black-eyed peas and collard greens out here?

BLACK SOLDIER *(Stunned)* I'm from Boston. *(Nixon hurries away to address the troops while the screen is filled with pictures of America's might)*

NIXON   I think that history will record that this may have been one of America's finest hours. *(Troops onstage start to mainline, puff pot, rag their officers, as Nixon hurries offstage)*

WASHINGTON   In the fall of 1969, the campuses were seething. Nixon was not ending the war. So a group of young activists decided to hold a series of moratoriums, to begin in October, with mass rallies, a peaceful form of protest . . .

NIXON   Under no circumstances will I be affected whatever.

WASHINGTON   Nevertheless, Nixon got busy. He fired General Hershey, the director of the draft; summoned home the ambassador to Saigon, and the ambassador to the Paris peace talks; announced he would deliver a major statement on the war by November third. He then sent the Vice President on a tour of the South, to say what ought to be said. The Vice President has for years been a student of the *Readers' Digest* section called "Increase Your Word Power." *(Agnew enters, ready for speechmaking)*

WASHINGTON   Agnew visited Mississippi.

AGNEW   A free government cannot impose rules of social acceptance upon its citizens. The point is this—in a man's private life he has the right to make his own friends. *(Rebel yells of delight)* For too long the South has been a punching bag for those who characterize themselves as liberal intellectuals . . . their course is one of applause for our enemies

(102)

and condemnation for our leaders. . . . The Republican Party has a place for every American who believes that flag waving is better than flag burning . . . *(More rebel yells,* applause)

WASHINGTON   The Vice President spoke in New Orleans.

AGNEW   A spirit of national masochism prevails, encouraged by an effete corps of impudent snobs who characterize themselves as intellectuals. *(Rebel yells, applause)*

WASHINGTON   The Vice President spoke in Harrisburg.

AGNEW   America is drifting toward Plato's classic definition of a degenerating democracy—a democracy that permits the voice of the mob to dominate the affairs of government. In the case of the Vietnam Moratorium, the objective announced by the leaders—immediate unilateral withdrawal—was not only unsound but idiotic. It is time to question the credentials of their leaders. If, in challenging, we polarize the American people, I say it is time for a positive polarization! We can afford to separate them from our society with no more regret than we should feel over discarding rotten apples from a barrel. *(Shots of the moratorium. The marches in Washington, etc.)*

WASHINGTON   For the young people, the moratorium was a great success. The President chose not to participate. Instead he announced that he was watching a football game on television. Then came November third. *(Nixon marches downstage to the TV camera. He is painted and aimed at the camera. He holds the Seal of the President like a shield)*

NIXON   Fifteen years ago North Vietnam, with the logistical support of Communist China and the Soviet Union, launched a campaign to impose a Communist government on South Vietnam by instigating and supporting a revolution . . . (*Washington waves: Nixon's mouth continues but the sound is off*)

WASHINGTON General Eisenhower . . . (*Eisenhower putts his way into view*) Do you believe that in 1954 North Vietnam launched a campaign to impose a Communist government on South Vietnam?

EISENHOWER . . . uh, ask Foster Dulles. He's somewhere around here . . . I'm not an expert in . . . uh, dates . . .

KENNEDY The answer is no. The concerned powers agreed that all foreign troops must leave Vietnam and that the entire country—North and South—hold a free election for President. The Eisenhower administration did not want this election to be held . . .

EISENHOWER President Diem didn't want it and we . . . uh, naturally . . .

WASHINGTON In your memoirs you were very candid, General.

EISENHOWER'S VOICE OVER I have never talked or corresponded with a person knowledgeable in Indo-Chinese affairs who did not agree that had elections been held as of the time of the fighting, possibly eighty percent of the population would have voted for the Communist Ho Chi Minh as their leader rather than chief of state Bao Dai.

EISENHOWER We could not allow that . . . of course . . .

WASHINGTON Then explain to me, gentlemen, if eighty percent of the people of North and South Vietnam wanted Ho Chi Minh for president, why couldn't they have him for president in a fair election?

KENNEDY   Ask Nixon. *(Washington waves)*

NIXON   We stand firm for the right of all the South Vietnamese people to determine for themselves the kind of government they want. *(Nixon looks happy. Speech is ended)*

WASHINGTON   A number of television commentators, among them Averell Harriman, thought that Nixon's speech had been singularly uninformative. Nixon was hurt. He ordered one of his writers to prepare a speech for Spiro Agnew to deliver at a dinner, previously turned down, in Des Moines, Iowa. *(Agnew trots onstage, raring to go)*

AGNEW   Where the President had issued a call for unity, Mr. Harriman was encouraging the country not to listen to him.

WASHINGTON   Mr. Agnew did not think the television commentators were representative of the silent majority.

AGNEW   *They* draw their social and political views from the same sources. Worse, they talk constantly to one another, thereby providing artificial reinforcement to their shared viewpoints.

WASHINGTON   Agnew seemed to think that television had invented the peace movement.

AGNEW   How many marches and demonstrations would we have if the marchers did not know that the ever-faithful TV cameras would be there to record their antics?

EISENHOWER   Who the hell is that?

WASHINGTON   Spiro Agnew. Nixon's Vice President.

EISENHOWER   If there's one thing I can't stand it's a Vice President.

KENNEDY   That is probably the only thing you and I will ever agree on.

(105)

WASHINGTON   Now Agnew makes his challenge to the television networks.

AGNEW   Whether what I've said to you tonight will be heard and seen at all by the nation is not my decision, it's not your decision, it's their decision. (*Agnew marches off-stage*)

KENNEDY   Only in America could a clown like that get on television in the first place.

WASHINGTON   The television networks were duly intimidated. Their licenses come from the government. More important, they make their money selling the products of manufacturers who fear controversy of any kind. The idea that television is in any way radical is perhaps the most ingenious creation of the Nixon fighting, socking, rocking tactics. As the next demonstration approached, Martha Mitchell, the wife of the Attorney General, made her contribution. (*Martha Mitchell, a bit high, scampers onstage*)

MARTHA   This place could become a complete fortress! You could have every building in Washington burned down. It could be a great, great catastrophe. And this is the thing I worried about way before I came to Washington, knowing the liberal element in this country is so, so against us. And my husband has said many times, some of the liberals in this country, he'd like to change them for the Russian Communists. (*She is gone*)

WASHINGTON   At first the Justice Department refused to grant the New Mobilization a permit to march, but the mayor of Washington persuaded the Department to grant a permit. (*On the screen the New Mobe—carrying the names of the war dead—pass in front of the White House, dropping the names into coffins, etc.*) For three days 300,-

ooo men and women, young and old, took part in what they called a March against Death. (*More shots of the New Mobe*) To the evident disappointment of the administration, the demonstration was largely peaceful.

MARTHA'S VOICE OVER   My husband made the comment to me, looking out the Justice Department, it looked like the Russian revolution going on.

WASHINGTON   Television took Agnew's warning to heart. The national networks devoted less than five minutes to live coverage of the three hundred thousand who demonstrated.

AGNEW'S VOICE OVER   Somehow when I look around the tube from time to time, I feel that I've had a modicum of success . . .

WASHINGTON   An Army private revealed on television that a massacre of Vietnamese civilians had taken place at a village called My Lai. (*During the next speech, shots of the slaughter at My Lai on screen*)

MEADLO'S VOICE OVER   There was about forty to forty-five people that we gathered in the center of the village—men, women, children, babies. And we all huddled them up. Lieutenant Calley started shooting them. And he told me to start shooting. So I started shooting. I poured about four clips into the group. I fired them on automatic. You just spray the area—so you can't know how many you killed. I must have killed ten or fifteen of them. So we started to gather them up, more people and we had seven or eight people—we put them in the hootch and we dropped a hand grenade in there with them—they had about seventy or seventy-five people all gathered up. So we threw ours in with them and Lieutenant Calley started pushing them off into the ravine. It was a ditch. And so we just pushed them off and just started using automatics on them—men, women, children and babies. After I done it, I felt good, but later on that day it was gettin' to me. It just seemed like it was the natural thing to do at the time.

WASHINGTON Lieutenant Calley's comment . . .

CALLEY'S VOICE OVER It was no big deal. *(Nixon enters with press interviewers)*

INTERVIEWER What about My Lai?

NIXON What appears was certainly a massacre and un der no circumstances was it justified.

WASHINGTON On the domestic front, Nixon was faced with a Supreme Court vacancy. He nominated a Southern judge named Haynsworth—who had been guilty of a conflict of interests. The Senate was not pleased with his record and said so.

NIXON *(Frowning)* I have examined the charges. I find that Judge Haynsworth is an honest man. I find that he has been, in my opinion, as a lawyer, a lawyer's lawyer and a judge's judge. I think he will be a great credit to the Supreme Court and I am going to stand by him until he is confirmed. I trust he will be.

INTERVIEWER Do you know Judge Haynsworth personally?

NIXON *(Shakes his head)* In fact, my acquaintance with Judge Haynsworth can only be casual. If he would walk into this room I am afraid I wouldn't recognize him.

WASHINGTON Haynsworth never did walk into that room. The Senate rejected him. Nixon then picked another Southerner. Judge Carswell.

NIXON *(Tightly)* The President is the one person en trusted by the Constitution with the power of appoint ment.

(108)

WASHINGTON   Apparently Nixon had not read the Constitution. Though the President may propose a judge to the Supreme Court, it is the Senate which must confirm the choice. The Senate was now in an angry mood. Judge Carswell's record was considered an insult to the Court and to the Senate. Even Senator Fulbright of Arkansas was outraged. Not only was Carswell an inept judge, but he had made the mistake of declaring in a political campaign that he was a devotee of white supremacy, then and forevermore. The Senate rejected him. Nixon was furious. Martha Mitchell was furious. At two in the morning she rang the editor of the Arkansas *Gazette* . . .

MARTHA'S VOICE OVER   I want you to crucify Fulbright and that's that!

WASHINGTON   Nixon then addressed himself to the South.

NIXON   I hope that the day will come when men like Judges Haynsworth and Carswell can and will sit on the High Court. As long as the Senate is constituted the way it is today, I will not nominate another Southerner and let him be subjected to the kind of malicious character assassination accorded both Judges Haynsworth and Carswell.

INTERVIEWER   Mr. President, would you have nominated Judge Carswell if you had known that he was a racist?

NIXON   Yes, I would. I'm not concerned about what Judge Carswell said twenty-four years ago when he was a candidate for state legislature . . .

WASHINGTON   In January 1970 Nixon gave his State of the Union message. *(Nixon solemnly holds up the Presidential Seal; peers over it)*

NIXON We must balance our Federal budget so that American families will have a better chance to balance their family budgets.

KENNEDY Oh, boy! He'll have to live with that one.

NIXON We had a balanced budget in 1969. This administration cut more than seven billion dollars out of spending plans in order to produce a surplus in 1970.

WASHINGTON In 1970 there was no surplus. The deficit was 19.1 billion dollars.

NIXON In spite of the fact that Congress reduced revenues by three billion dollars, I can recommend a balanced budget for 1971.

WASHINGTON The deficit for 1971 will be one of the largest in national history, over twenty-three billion dollars. (*Nixon has finished his speech. He sits at his desk, quietly pleased with himself*)

Nixon took a very special view of presidential commissions. If what they recommended was contrary to what he wanted them to recommend he would either reject their findings or appoint a new commission to report to him what he wanted to hear. His commission on oil proposed that the United States import foreign oil, as it was cheaper than domestic oil. Loyal to his old backers, he appointed a second commission. They decided *not* to import foreign oil. As for the commission on pornography . . .

NIXON That was Johnson's commission, not mine.

WASHINGTON The commission found that pornography was not harmful.

NIXON So long as I am in the White House, there will be no relaxation of the national effort to control and eliminate smut from national life.

WASHINGTON   Nixon appointed a commission to decide whether or not to legalize marijuana, but no matter what the commission proposes . . .

NIXON   I am against the proposals that are made to legalize marijuana. I believe that, in the long run, that would be a very detrimental policy for this country, and certainly detrimental to the young people of this country, because it's only a halfway house to something worse.

WASHINGTON   Nixon is a renowned mixer of dry martinis. (*Nixon nods proudly*)

During this period Nixon, in the now-familiar pattern of recent Presidents, was conducting a secret war in Laos. But since it was not convenient to admit this, he announced . . . (*Shots of American activity in Laos*)

NIXON   There are no American ground combat troops in Laos. We have no plans for introducing ground combat forces in Laos. No American stationed in Laos has ever been killed in ground combat operations.

WASHINGTON   The legalistic cover phrase is "ground combat." Unfortunately for Nixon, at least one American, Captain John Bush, had been killed in ground combat the year before. (*Nixon goes offstage during this, leaving a press aide to confront a reporter*)

AIDE   Captain Bush was in his quarters, in the compound ten miles to the rear of the expected line of contact with the enemy in Laos when North Vietnamese commandos attacked the compound. Captain Bush took action immediately to attempt to protect other persons in the compound, exposing himself to enemy fire and was killed. He was not engaged in combat operations, he died as a result of hostile action . . .

(111)

INTERVIEWER   But since Captain Bush was shooting at enemy commandos on the night of February 11, 1969, then he was engaged in combat, on the ground . . . *(The aide flees. Enter Nixon ready for press conference)*

WASHINGTON   In March 1970, the President held one of his rare press conferences. *(Nixon stands before the press)*

INTERVIEWER   I am wondering how you feel about the recent developments in Cambodia and how it relates to our activities in Vietnam?

WASHINGTON   The government of Prince Sihanouk has just been deposed by a right-wing military junta.

NIXON   These developments in Cambodia are quite difficult to appraise . . . I will simply say that we respect Cambodia's neutrality.

INTERVIEWER   As a California voter how do you feel about the disclosure that Senator Murphy remains on the Technicolor payroll, and the entry of Mr. Simon in the race?

NIXON   Well, as a California voter, I intend to vote for Senator Murphy if he wins the nomination, and I expect him to win it.

INTERVIEWER   One of the key issues in the country seems to be still inflation . . .

NIXON   I am confident that the policies that we are following have taken the fire out of the inflation.

INTERVIEWER   Unemployment?

NIXON   The rate of unemployment at the present time is 4.2 percent.

WASHINGTON   Actually it is 4.4 percent. By January first it will be six percent.

INTERVIEWER   Recession?

NIXON   One, this country is not in a recession at the present time. Second, this is an activist administration. We are going to take action to avoid a recession at the same time that we are taking action to cool the fires of inflation. Three, 1970 is going to be a good year from an economic standpoint. *(A patter of applause from the journalists. Nixon picks up military cap and tries it on. A single reporter confronts him)*

REPORTER   What exactly will the government do about desegregating schools in the South?

NIXON   In achieving desegregation we must proceed with the least possible disruption of the education of the nation's children . . . de facto racial separation resulting genuinely from housing patterns exists in the South as well as the North; in neither area should this condition by itself be cause for federal enforcement actions.

REPORTER   How far do you plan to go in using federal powers to promote racial integration in suburban housing?

NIXON   Only to the extent that the law requires . . . I believe that forced integration of the suburbs is not in the national interest. *(Exit reporter. Martial music begins)*

WASHINGTON   Referring to the new government in Cambodia, the Secretary of State said, on April 12 . . .

SECRETARY'S VOICE OVER   Our best policy is to be as quiet as possible, to avoid any act which appears to violate the neutrality of Cambodia.

WASHINGTON   For more than a year Nixon had been withdrawing troops from Vietnam. He had indicated to Hanoi that eventually all American troops would go. Though he spoke of Vietnamization of the war—which meant that what the South Vietnamese army could not do with the aid of a half-million American troops they would be able to do alone—he had made it clear that he was winding down the war. He then expected a settlement with Hanoi. But Hanoi had nothing to gain by a settlement and everything to gain by simply waiting for Nixon and the legions to depart, as Nixon had said they would. Nixon's policy was a failure. On April twenty-third the Secretary of State told Congress . . .

SECRETARY'S VOICE OVER   We recognize that if we escalate and we get involved in Cambodia with our ground troops, then our whole program is defeated.

WASHINGTON   One week later Nixon invaded Cambodia. *(Shots of Cambodia being invaded; of campuses responding. Nixon addresses the nation)*

NIXON   Tonight American and South Vietnamese units will attack the headquarters for the entire Communist military operations in South Vietnam. This key control center has been occupied by the North Vietnamese and Viet Cong for five years in blatant violation of Cambodia's neutrality. This is not an invasion of Cambodia . . .

WASHINGTON   It later developed that there was no important Communist headquarters in Cambodia, and never had been.

NIXON   A majority of the American people want to keep the casualties of our brave men in Vietnam at an absolute minimum. The action I take tonight is essential if we are to accomplish that goal.

EISENHOWER *(Startled)*   Hey! I must've missed something there . . . did he say he's going to keep down casualties by *invading* Cambodia . . .

(114)

KENNEDY   Yes. He wants us to believe that if he doesn't go into Cambodia, the last American troops to get onto the troop ships will be massacred by North Vietnamese troops from a sanctuary in Cambodia.

EISENHOWER   That makes no sense.

KENNEDY   No, it does not.

WASHINGTON   But this speech is very revelatory—of the man if not the situation.

NIXON   If when the chips are down the world's most powerful nation, the United States of America, acts like a pitiful, helpless giant, the forces of totalitarianism and anarchy will threaten free nations and free institutions throughout the world.

EISENHOWER   I don't like that word "helpless . . ."

KENNEDY   Is this the speech where he used the word "humiliation" three times?

WASHINGTON   Yes. I'm afraid Nixon knows what it is to be humiliated . . . by masters.

EISENHOWER   Don't look at me . . . I always treated him the way . . . uh, he ought to be treated.

NIXON   Others are saying that today this move against the enemy sanctuaries will make me a one-term President . . .

KENNEDY   My God, men are dying and he talks about his political career!

WASHINGTON   He is just more naked than the rest of you.

NIXON   Whether I may be a one-term President is insignificant compared to whether by our failure to act in this crisis the United States proves itself to be unworthy to lead the forces of freedom in this critical period in world history. I would rather be a one-term President and do what I believe is right than to be a two-term President at the cost of seeing America become a second-rate power . . .

KENNEDY   If I were he I would insist on getting back every penny I paid that psychiatrist.

EISENHOWER   Dick never did have much . . . uh, dignity.

KENNEDY   One good thing . . . he's made it obligatory for the American people to see to it that he really is a one-term President. *(A Senator enters, crosses to Nixon)*

SENATOR   Mr. President, world opinion is against you, particularly in Europe. The Soviet has said . . .

NIXON   We expect the Soviets to protest this, just as we protested the Soviet invasion of Czechoslovakia. *(Stunned, the Senator withdraws)*

EISENHOWER   You know, he might be a little . . . uh, unhinged . . . Dick always did say some of the damndest things . . .

KENNEDY   Believe me, I prefer his lies to his truths.

WASHINGTON   To Nixon's apparent surprise, there was a wave of revulsion against him and the widening of the war. At Kent State University in Ohio, National Guardsmen shot and killed three students as they demonstrated against the war . . . *(On screen the shootings at Kent State)* The President at first had no comment about the three murders. Then he was inspired to say . . .

NIXON   This should remind us all once again that when dissent turns to violence it invites tragedy.

WASHINGTON   When it became clear that the dissenters of Kent State had *not* turned to violence, Nixon elaborated . . .

(116)

NIXON   You know, you see these bums—you know, blowing up the campuses. Listen, the boys on the college campuses today are the luckiest people in the world, going to the greatest universities, and here they are burning up the books, I mean storming around about this issue. I mean you name it, get rid of the war. There'll be another one . . .

WASHINGTON   A week later Nixon recanted—somewhat . . .

NIXON   I would certainly regret that my use of the word "bums" was interpreted to apply to those who dissent . . . When students on university campuses burn buildings, engage in violence, break up furniture, terrorize their fellow students and the faculty, then I think "bums" is perhaps too kind a word to apply to that kind of person. Those are the kind I was referring to.

INTERVIEWER   Have you been surprised by the intensity of the protest, and will it affect your policy?

NIXON   No, I have not been surprised by the intensity of the protest. I realize that those who are protesting . . . (*His mouth continues to move; sound is off*)

WASHINGTON   But Nixon *was* astonished by the violence of the response to his invasion of a neutral country. He went on television. He defended himself. Meanwhile Washington was filled with the young and angry . . . (*Shots of young protesters at the Memorial, the Ellipse, etc.*)

After the press conference, Nixon could not sleep. He telephoned people most of the night. He spoke of his love for the young.

NIXON   Why, I really love these kids. I've told Haldeman and Ehrlichman to bring them in, I want to see them all.

(Against a background of the Lincoln Memorial, Nixon approaches young people, shakes hands; they are stunned)

WASHINGTON   Nixon tries to talk to the young.

NIXON'S VOICE OVER   I told them how in 1939 I thought that Neville Chamberlain was the greatest man living and that Winston Churchill was a madman. It was not until years later that I realized that Churchill was right. I doubt if that got over.

NIXON *(To students)*   I know you think we are a bunch of sons of bitches . . . *(Loud agreement)* I know you want to get the war over. Sure you came here to demonstrate and shout your slogans on the Ellipse. That's all right. Have a good time in Washington, and don't go away bitter.

STUDENT   Mr. President, we come from a very uptight university . . .

NIXON   Which one?

STUDENT   Syracuse.

NIXON   How's the football team doing this year? *(Nixon moves on. Eyes down)* Where are you from?

STUDENT   California.

NIXON   Get in any surfing this spring?

FIRST STUDENT *(To the audience)*   All the students that were standing around were amazed, they were in shock, because they couldn't believe that this man was the President of the United States. What he was saying just absolutely made no sense . . .

NIXON   Tucson has nice hills. You should travel while you're still young. Japan, Mexico, China—if possible—Indo-China, India, Iran, the Soviet Union, Hungary, Czechoslovakia . . .

(118)

SECOND STUDENT *(To the audience)* We reacted as if he was mad, you know, like he needed help. I mean I was in just utter disbelief. I think he just needs a rest. You know, maybe that's the nicest way to put it. He has no conception of how important these issues are and he, you know, he's just in a fog . . .

NIXON Japan, Mexico, China—if possible . . .

THIRD STUDENT *(To the audience)* He seemed very tired and nervous and, you know, he was all leaning over, and he was looking at the floor, he couldn't look at anybody, he looked like he had make-up all over his face, and he seemed very scared, really . . .

NIXON Have a nice day . . . have a nice day . . . *(Nixon is shaking hands and exiting)*

FIRST STUDENT *(To the audience)* He just kept saying "have a really nice day, have a really nice time," and then he said there wouldn't be any trouble, which was a blatant lie, since he gassed all the people at the Monument . . . *(Nixon is gone. Students look shell-shocked. Then they vanish)*

WASHINGTON A month after the invasion of Cambodia, Nixon declared a great victory and withdrew American troops.

NIXON I can now state that this has been the most successful operation of this long and very difficult war. *(Agnew enters)*

AGNEW We captured a laundry facility and a large store of freshly laundered uniforms. *(Exit Agnew)*

WASHINGTON Unfortunately they had not been able to find the headquarters of the entire Communist high command, but they did find some rice, medical supplies and a few captured enemy documents.

KENNEDY To be turned over to Joe Alsop.

WASHINGTON   At the time of the invasion, only a small part of Cambodia was under Communist control. After the invasion, two thirds of the country was under Communist control.

EISENHOWER   It's difficult to see exactly what he's trying to do . . .

KENNEDY   Difficult? He's getting the same line from the Generals we used to get.

EISENHOWER   I never listened to Pentagon Generals . . . Didn't have to . . .

KENNEDY   Well, I had to. So does he. Note the way he keeps talking about "ground combat troops." And how casualties, which were running several hundred a week under Johnson, are now "only fourteen." His plan is to remove all ground troops by '72 but keep the Air Force and the logistical forces in Vietnam.

EISENHOWER   That doesn't square with all this talk about getting out . . .

KENNEDY   He has no intention of getting out. Ever. He wants to reduce casualties so that the American people will forget we're still involved in what he calls Vietnamization.

WASHINGTON   Would you have done the same?

KENNEDY   Well . . . I was convinced we should remain on the Asian continent.

EISENHOWER   So was I . . . but no infantry battles, no guerrilla warfare, no Green Beret nonsense . . .

KENNEDY *(Stung)*   For your information, the Green Berets . . .

WASHINGTON *(Quiets them)*   The congressional elections of 1970 were beginning. The President began in a mood of statesmanlike magnanimity. Even the Vice President was benign . . .

AGNEW'S VOICE OVER I would hope that all the members of the administration would have in mind a rule that I have always had, and it's a very simple one, when the action is hot keep the rhetoric cool.

WASHINGTON But there were lapses, as early as August. On a trip to California the President looked at the local newspapers. *(Shots of Manson, family, murders)* Charles Manson and "family" were on trial for the alleged murder of a number of people. In New Orleans, the President made a number of verbal fluffs. *(Nixon beams at crowd)*

NIXON I first visited New Orleans in 1941, and I want to thank you for welcoming somebody that was nothing, as I was twenty-nine years ago. *(Cheers)* Instead of just sitting in Washington waiting for the people to come there, we are bringing the White House to all over the country. And now it is right here—in Washington D.C. *(Aides mutter "New Orleans" but Nixon does not hear)*

KENNEDY Does he drink?

EISENHOWER How should I know? Never saw that much of him.

NIXON Young people glorify wrongdoers perhaps because of the dramatic attention criminals get in TV and in the press.

WASHINGTON Both President and Vice President seem to think that the press is in some way responsible for all the crimes it reports.

NIXON I noted for example the coverage of the Charles Manson case when I was in Los Angeles, front page every day in the papers.

(121)

KENNEDY   He's jealous. Maybe he should kill Pat, Tricia, Julie and David and get some real headlines.

NIXON *(Poisonous look at Kennedy)*   It usually goes a couple of minutes in the evening news. Here is a man who is guilty, directly or indirectly, of eight murders without reason . . .

WASHINGTON   Since Manson had not yet been found guilty, Nixon was criticized for prejudicing Manson's chance of a fair trial . . .

NIXON *(Plaintively)*   I said charged. Didn't I?

AIDE   No, Mr. President.

WASHINGTON   In October Nixon's alleged shrink, Dr. Hutschnecker, billed as a theorist in thought-behavior control, wrote an article in *The New York Times,* entitled "A Plea for Experiments." He wanted federal or private money in order to conduct experiments on as many six-year-olds as possible to determine whether or not they had delinquent tendencies. They were then to be observed and treated over the years by what he called "parapsychologists." The White House seemed to take to this plan until it was shot down by angry parents, not to mention bona-fide psychiatrists —on the ground that *all* six-year-olds have delinquent tendencies. A month before the election, Nixon took another swift tour of Europe. Then he addressed the nation on his new initiative for peace in Southeast Asia. *(Nixon holds up the Great Seal: stares into camera)*

NIXON   As you know, I have just returned from a trip which took me to Italy, Spain, Yugoslavia, England, Ireland. Hundreds of thousands of people cheered me as I drove through the cities of those countries.

KENNEDY Try driving through the Bronx, through Harlem . . . *(Nixon puts down the Seal. Starts to campaign)*

WASHINGTON There was nothing new in Nixon's new initiative for peace, but it sounded as though he was doing something, which was useful, since there was an election a few weeks later. *(Signs of impending election. "The American People" are delivered to center stage. Nixon mounts a pedestal. Agnew is at the base. A couple of hippie-type demonstrators approach. Nixon looks serene, presidential)*

AGNEW *(Points to hippies)* They're devoid of intelligence. They really don't belong on a college campus. They belong in some place where they can receive some remedial instructions. *(Nixon smiles)* No small group of self-designated elitists who don't know enough to come out of the rain in a deluge has a right to tell *(Points to Nixon)* him how to run this country. *(Nixon smiles and raises his arms—in victory. But "The American People" are inching away from him. Several young people approach)*

THE YOUNG One, two, three, four—we don't like your fucking war! *(Nixon looks slightly flustered. Agnew helps a TV cameraman aim his lens at the young: it is important that the silent majority see the sort of obscene heckling their President gets)* Five, six, seven, eight—we don't want a Fascist state!

AGNEW *(Indicates the young)* It's time to sweep that kind of garbage out of our society.

WASHINGTON At Burlington, Vermont, one piece of cement about the size of a dollar bill was thrown at the President's plane. It fell short of its target. That was the limit of rock-throwing.

NIXON Let me say that I respect their right to be heard even if they do not respect my right to be heard. The time has come for the silent majority to stand up and be c ounted against the rock throwers!

WASHINGTON Not only was the President on the attack against those Democrats who wanted to end the war, he was also out to purge at least one Republican Senator who opposed the war, Goodell of New York . . .

AGNEW Goodell is the Christine Jorgensen of the Republican Party. *(Nixon makes the OK sign at Agnew)*

WASHINGTON In California Nixon challenged the hecklers. He climbed on top of a car and made the victory sign . . . *(Nixon mimes all this. On the screen, shots of the mobs at San José)*

NIXON That's what they hate to see! *("The American People" are inching farther away. The young throw a few pebbles in Nixon's direction: he is not touched)*

ROSEMARY WOOD'S VOICE OVER This is just like Caracas!

NIXON There is no cause that justifies the use of violence or lawlessness.

THE YOUNG That's what we've been trying to tell you about Vietnam. *(Nixon pretends not to hear)*

WASHINGTON The Republicans lost nine seats in the House, eleven governorships, and gained two and a half seats in the Senate. *(Nixon is at his desk)* Nineteen Republican Senators denounced Nixon and Agnew for their attacks upon Senator Goodell—who was defeated.

NIXON The election, ideologically, was enormously successful.

WASHINGTON The President now assumed his statesman's mantle.

(124)

INTERVIEWER   How do you reconcile your comments on the Manson case with your status as a lawyer?

NIXON   I think that's a legitimate criticism. I think sometimes we lawyers, even like doctors who try to prescribe for themselves, may make mistakes. And I think that kind of comment probably is unjustified.

KENNEDY   He admitted to making a mistake—that is very unpresidential.

WASHINGTON   John Mitchell, the Attorney General, analyzed the mood of the nation.

MITCHELL'S VOICE OVER   This country is going so far right that you are not even going to recognize it.

WASHINGTON   The President's press secretary was asked about rumors that Nixon might not run again.

KLEIN'S VOICE OVER   You just don't know the man. Richard Nixon simply loves being President of the United States. (*Nixon, at his desk, nods happily*)

WASHINGTON   Nixon discusses Pat. (*Pat appears during this, beaming, with a mop and bucket. She cleans the floor as he talks of her*)

NIXON   Any lady who is First Lady likes being First Lady. I don't care what they say. They like it. All Presidents have very grave problems. The wife has to be the stronger partner of the two. (*Shots of Women's Lib on screen. Nixon toys with the butterfly net*) I don't believe that on any issue you can have the wife talking one way and the husband talking another way. (*Nixon picks up a cup of coffee from the desk*) She is very strict about keeping the place clean. (*Nixon pours coffee on floor. Beaming, Pat mops it up*) When you spill a cup of coffee on the floor, she is down there scrubbing it . . . she keeps, and always wants, the place to be ship-shape.

WASHINGTON   While Pat is cleaning up around the White House, Tricia has been thinking about politics.
TRICIA'S VOICE OVER   The Vice President is incredible. It's amazing what he has done to the media, helping them to reform themselves. You can't underestimate the power of fear. (*Nixon nods happily*)
WASHINGTON   The State of the Union speech promised a new American revolution. (*Nixon is on his feet, clutches the Seal. Addresses Congress*)
NIXON   A revolution as profound, as far-reaching, as exciting as that first revolution almost two hundred years ago . . .
WASHINGTON   This revolution was to come about as the result of sharing federal revenue with the states, except of course there was nothing to share but a nineteen-billion-dollar deficit . . .
NIXON   The tide of inflation has turned. The rise in the cost of living, which has been gathering momentum in the late sixties, was reduced last year . . .
WASHINGTON   Actually it increased by 6.2 percent.
NIXON   Inflation will be further reduced this year.
WASHINGTON   Inflation will increase in 1971 at the rate of 3.9 percent.
NIXON   We should take no comfort from the fact that the level of unemployment in this transition from a wartime to a peactime economy is lower than in any peacetime year of the 1960s.
WASHINGTON   They *should* take no comfort since the level of unemployment is higher than any year of the 1960s except 1961.
NIXON   It will be a full-employment budget, a budget designed to be in balance if the economy were operating at

its peak potential. By spending as if we were at full employment, we will help to bring about full employment.

WASHINGTON Every day and in every way, better and better. To date, under this plan, unemployment has gone to over six percent. In cities like Seattle it is now over ten percent.

NIXON I do not plan to ask for wage and price controls.

WASHINGTON Before going on the air, the President shaves and jogs in place to bring the color to his cheeks. (*Nixon mimes all this. Then a make-up man paints him*) In January, Nixon had a chat on television with Howard K. Smith. Just before the broadcast, Nixon confided to Smith . . . (*Nixon sits in an easy chair. Camera next to him*)

NIXON I am now a Keynesian in economics.

SMITH (*To the audience*) That's a little like a Christian Crusader saying, "All things considered, I think Mohammed was right."

WASHINGTON Later when Smith asked him why it was that people in his own Cabinet had such difficulty in seeing him—that they were usually shunted off to lesser White House aides—Nixon said . . .

NIXON I think there is no substitute, Mr. Smith, for seeing the man in the Oval Office, and yet while my schedule, as you probably are aware, due to a rather disciplined schedule unless I have a guest, I eat breakfast alone in five minutes, never have guests for lunch—I do that in five minutes, too. I perhaps put more time in in the day than any President could put in, and it is because it is my way and not bragging about it.

WASHINGTON Lieutenant Calley was found guilty of the murders at My Lai. (*Shots of the trial, Calley, demon-*

strations) There was a great popular outcry in favor of Calley. The right wing saw nothing wrong in shooting gooks of any kind. The left wing thought Calley was a scapegoat, and that the real murderers were Johnson, Westmoreland, Nixon. The White House responded . . .

NIXON Before any final sentence is carried out—the President will personally review the case and finally decide it.

WASHINGTON The Code of Military Justice does not of course provide for any appeal to the President, nor any mandatory review by the President . . .

NIXON Not strictly legal in nature but since the case has captured the interest of the American people, I shall assert the inherent powers as commander-in-chief . . .

WASHINGTON (*To Nixon*) Can it be predicted what sort of "nonlegal" considerations will be involved?

NIXON (*Gravely*) This is sort of in the heart of a man.

INTERVIEWER What do you feel about the press?

NIXON I have never called a publisher, never called an editor, never called a reporter. I don't care. And, you know, that's what makes them mad. That's what infuriates them. I just don't care.

INTERVIEWER What is your view of Women's Lib?

NIXON I am not an expert in these things. But my view is, don't be too concerned about the fact that women don't have an equal chance. They do all right in this town.

INTERVIEWER What women have you appointed to high office . . . ? (*But Nixon changes the subject*)

NIXON As for the family . . . (*Frowns, thinking hard*) As we see, frankly, life is becoming perhaps less demanding . . . (*On the screen, shots of poverty in Mississippi, Harlem,*

Appalachia) Less demanding in the sense that it is possible now for most people to get a job . . . *(Shots of the unemployed in Seattle, L.A., New York)*

The tendency there is to affect the family, and particularly young people, in a way that they move away from principle, from values, and are at somewhat loose ends . . . Some way we have failed to have our young people feel that this is a good time to be alive and not a bad time to be alive . . . *(Shots of the young being beaten in Chicago, Washington, L.A.)* And if you had to choose a place to live, this is the best country in the world in which to live.

WASHINGTON   According to a recent Gallup Poll, sixteen million Americans would like to emigrate. Preferably to Australia . . . On July third, the President addressed the nation. *(Nixon gathers up the Seal)*

NIXON   To look at America with clear eyes today is to see every reason for pride and little for shame . . . *(On the screen, shots of Vietnam, Cambodia, Laos, ruined forests, civilian dead . . . and statistics superimposed: one million Vietnamese civilians dead as a result of American bombing, 6 million made refugees, etc.)* . . . great cause for gratitude and little for regret, strong grounds for hope and none at all for despair. *(During this, shots of poverty—people in Appalachia, blacks, Chicanos. Statistics superimposed: twenty-five million Americans at the poverty level, etc.)* The crucial challenge now is to hold the high ground of confidence, courage and faith that is rightly ours and to avoid the quicksand of fear and doubt.

WASHINGTON   In the spirit of the Fourth of July—his, may I say, and not mine—he chose to ignore the millions of Americans out of work, the millions who will never find work, chose to ignore the disaster in Southeast Asia, where a mutinous army ridden with drugs is on its way home, looking for work that does not exist. The President ignored the state of the environment, the rivers that catch fire, the lakes in which nothing lives, the air poisoned by factories and automobiles— none of these things concerned the President last July Fourth because . . .

NIXON   The time has come to answer the false charge that this is an ugly country. Let us love America. Let us love her not because she is strong and not because she is rich, but because America is a good country and we can make her better. *(Nixon picks up the Seal of the President of the United States and walks to the wings. He pauses. Turns to the audience)* I shall go to China. *(Sound of "Chopsticks" being played. Nixon is gone)*

VOICE OVER   The American international trade balance for 1971 is the worst since 1893. The value of the 1957–59 dollar fell during the Nixon administration from 80.6 cents to 70.8 cents.

NIXON'S VOICE OVER   I am today ordering a freeze on all prices and wages throughout the United States for a period of ninety days.

VOICE OVER   When the American Bar Association—or ABA—turned down Nixon's next pair of Supreme Court Justices, the President said . . .

NIXON'S VOICE OVER   Fuck the ABA. *(Kennedy and Eisenhower and Washington look at one another—slightly dazed. The cherry tree is in the background)*

EISENHOWER   Well . . . that was, uh, not a bad speech, as that sort of thing goes, lots of things wrong of course at home but . . .

KENNEDY   He'll go to *China!* He'll go to the moon. Anything to get out of that good country of ours. *(Shakes his head)* Think how he'd have crucified me if I'd said I was going to China. *(Mimics)* "I don't doubt President Kennedy's loyalty but . . ."

EISENHOWER   You know, watching this, I can't say . . . I mean I don't see any great . . . well, *consistency* to Dick's career . . .

WASHINGTON   It would seem to me that the only thing which consistently interests him is running for office and getting elected.

KENNEDY *(Ironically)*   A very wise, a very perceptive statement, General Washington.

WASHINGTON   Am I to infer from your tone that I am naïve?

KENNEDY   What else *consistently* interests any of us?

EISENHOWER   Never thought I'd hear *you* admit it.

KENNEDY *(To Washington)*   Wasn't it true of you, General?

WASHINGTON   The first time, I was chosen President unanimously. The second time . . . the Presidency was a painful burden, and I was glad to set it down, with a message to those who came after . . . I prayed that we may be always prepared for war but never unsheathe the sword except in self-defense . . .

KENNEDY   But what is self-defense?

EISENHOWER   Yes, if Laos falls, Vietnam falls, Thailand falls. Eventually we'll have to fight them in California . . .

WASHINGTON   Fight who?

EISENHOWER   Well, the . . . uh, the Chinese, I suppose . . . you know, or somebody like that . . .

WASHINGTON It will be many years before the Chinese achieve military parity with the United States . . .

KENNEDY General, it is our normal instinct to try to dominate others. I am surprised you were not aware of it when you made your farewell address.

WASHINGTON I was. I was also aware that those who try to conquer the world usually fail, which would be a good and fair thing were it not that their people and its best institutions are often destroyed in the process, and that is a bad thing, which is why I said: nothing is more essential than that permanent inveterate antipathies against particular nations and passionate attachments for others should be *excluded.* I believed in our interest first, but guided by justice. Since neither of you gentlemen believed in justice, you could not, finally, promote the best interest of the Republic. So here we are tonight. With a lost war. A declining economy. A bitter polity . . .

EISENHOWER *(Stops him)* General, we deal with such a small space of history at a time—things are in motion when we arrive—so, like it or not we have to move *with* events. Some of us keep the peace better than others, but nothing more. Anyway, you came at the beginning. You were lucky. We came at the . . . we came later in the story.

KENNEDY I wanted a just society but I thought it could not be done if we gave up our empire, and empires, no matter how achieved, are dangerous things to let go.

EISENHOWER Who's *that* from?

KENNEDY   From the funeral oration of Pericles to his people, on the subject of their dead, killed by a long war.

WASHINGTON   As of tonight, how many people do you think have been killed, wounded, made homeless in the name of the United States of America? *(Neither Kennedy nor Eisenhower responds. A long moment)*

VOICE OVER   George, who cut down that cherry tree?

KENNEDY *(Promptly)*   Nixon did.

VOICE OVER   *Who* did?

EISENHOWER   Now we gotta be fair about that one. We . . . uh, we all did! *(Then, suddenly, jubilant music: Washington, Eisenhower, Kennedy grab hands gaily as the cast runs onstage, and to a happy jazzy version of the national anthem, they dance while on the screen "by the rockets' red glare" we see bombs exploding in Asia, the flag in shreds, as the curtain falls)*

Sources

Bibliography

Adler, Bill: *The Wit and Humor of Richard Nixon* (New York, Popular Library, 1969).

Alsop, Stewart: *Nixon and Rockefeller: A Double Portrait* (New York, Doubleday, 1960).

Costello, William: *The Facts about Nixon, an Unauthorized Biography* (New York, The Viking Press, 1960).

Democratic National Committee, Washington, D.C.: "What Nixon Said," a compilation of Nixon quotations.

de Toledano, Ralph: *One Man Alone: Richard Nixon* (New York, Funk & Wagnalls, 1969).

Drury, Allen: *Courage and Hesitation* (New York, Doubleday, 1971).

Effros, William G., ed.: *Quotations Vietnam: 1945–1970* (New York, Random House, 1970).

Evans, Rowland, Jr., and Robert D. Novak: *Nixon in the White House: The Frustration of Power* (New York, Random House, 1971).

Harris, Mark: *Mark the Glove Boy* (New York, Macmillan, 1964).

Keogh, James: *This Is Nixon* (New York, G.P. Putnam's, 1956).

Kornitzer, Bela: *The Real Nixon, An Intimate Biography* (Chicago, Rand McNally & Co., 1960).

McGinniss, Joe: *The Selling of the President 1968* (New York, Pocket Books, 1970).

Mazo, Earl: *Richard Nixon, A Political and Personal Portrait* (New York, Harper & Brothers, 1959).

Mazo, Earl and Stephen Hess: *Nixon, A Political Portrait* (New York, Harper & Row, 1968).

Nixon, Richard M.: *Six Crises* (Garden City, N.Y., Doubleday & Co., 1962).

Osborne, John: *The Second Year of the Nixon Watch* (New York, Liveright, 1971).

Rovere, Richard H.: *The Eisenhower Years* (New York, Farrar, Straus, and Cudahy, 1956).

Schnapper, M.B., ed.: *Quotations from the Would-Be Chairman Poor Richard Nixon's Very Own Words* (Washington, D.C., Public Affairs Press, 1968).

Shepherd, Jack and Christopher S. Wren, eds.: *The Almanack of Poor Richard Nixon* (Cleveland and New York, The World Publishing Co., 1968).

The Nixon-Agnew Campaign Committee: *Nixon on the Issues* (New York, October 17, 1968).

White, Theodore H.: *The Making of the President 1968* (New York, Atheneum Publishers, 1969).

The Making of the President 1960 (New York, Atheneum Publishers, 1961).

Wills, Gary: *Nixon Agonistes, The Crisis of the Self-Made Man* (Boston, Houghton Mifflin Company, 1970).

Witcover, Jules: *The Resurrection of Richard Nixon* (New York, G.P. Putnam's Sons, 1970).

Sources

Phase One

Page 8   "It is true that we had hardships . . ." Kornitzer, pp. 35–36.

Page 9   "We were poor but . . ." *Ibid.*, p. 114.

            "We not only learned . . ." *Ibid.*, pp. 35–36.

            "That train whistle . . ." Mazo, p. 13.

            "I learned early that . . ." Kornitzer, p. 79.

Page 10   "Mother, I would like . . ." *Ibid.*, p. 19.

Page 11   "Picking string beans . . ." Paraphrased from Mazo, p. 15.

Page 12   "I'm scared . . ." *Ibid.*, p. 25.

Page 13   "I won my share . . ." Wills, p. 159.

Page 14   "General Eisenhower never asked me . . ." Paraphrased from Costello, p. 230; White, 1961, p. 72; Wills, p. 124.

            "Eisenhower was a far . . ." Nixon, p. 161.

Page 15   ". . . in the best sense . . ." *Ibid.*

            "If they had given me . . ." Mazo, p. 26.

Page 16   "When I just started law . . ." *Saturday Evening Post,* 7–12–58.

Page 17   "The worst thing . . ." Mazo, p. 5.

"A friend told me . . ." Kornitzer, p. 134.

"I'm going to marry you." Costello, p. 28.

Page 18   "At OPA, I saw that . . ." de Toledano, pp. 36–37.

". . . the boys who were then being trained . . ." Costello, p. 29.

"As a Quaker I could claim . . ." Paraphrased from de Toledano, pp. 36–37.

"I was sent to the Pacific . . ." Speech on NBC TV, 9–23–52 (Checkers speech).

Page 19   "I never knew what poker was . . ." Mazo, p. 37.

"Politics never occurred to me . . ." Paraphrased from Nixon, p. 298: "Nothing occurred in this period [early 1940's] to indicate a possible future political career."

Page 20   "I guess so." Rovere, p. 305.

"One, advocated by . . ." Costello, p. 40.

Page 21   "We will put on . . ." Pomona, California, 11–3–49, Shepherd and Wren, p. 16.

Page 23   "You were in favor . . ." Costello, p. 57.

"Grain rationing . . ." *Ibid.*

"Meat rationing . . ." *Ibid.*

"There are the people . . ." Costello, pp. 57–58.

"would deprive the people . . ." Costello, p. 58.

"Here is proof that . . ." Paraphrased from Costello's account of the debate, p. 53.

"At a meeting in Los Angeles . . ." *Ibid.*

Page 24   "Here is the proof!" *Ibid.*

"Communism was *not* the issue . . ." Costello, p. 53.

"No, nothing in particular." Washington, D.C., 1–3–47, New York *Post* 10–1–52.

"Politically, it can be . . ." de Toledano, p. 64.

Page 25   "The tragedy of this case . . ." *Congressional Record* 1–26–50.

"There were rumors that . . ." Mazo, p. 56.

". . . denied ever having heard . . ." Nixon, p. 7.

"If the American people . . ." de Toledano, p. 85.

"He was rather insolent . . ." Mazo, p. 56.

"Although we could not . . ." Mazo, p. 55.

Page 26   "The nation finally saw . . ." Nixon, p. 65.

"Communism in America . . ." *Ibid.*

"The Communist Hiss . . ." Nixon, p. 67.

"Our beliefs must be . . ." *Ibid.*, p. 68.

Page 27   "That is the most dishonest . . ." Costello, p. 61.

"I have been advised . . ." Costello, p. 63.

Page 28   "During the six years . . ." *Ibid.*

"My opponent did not vote . . ." Costello, pp. 68–69.

Page 30   "This is another typical smear . . ." Sacramento, California, 9–19–52, Shepherd and Wren, p. 45.

"I never said that . . ." Alsop, p. 196.

"We'll take care of people . . ." Costello, p. 6.

Page 31   "There are only two alternatives . . ." *Ibid.*, p. 81.

Page 32   "Wishful thinking . . ." Mazo, p. 295.

Page 33   "Folks! Haven't we got . . ." de Toledano, p. 136.

"Despite Ike's great capacity . . ." Nixon, p. 76.

"There has never been . . ." Mazo, p. 287.

"The plan was for General . . ." Wills, p. 87.

Page 34   "There he is! Adlai . . ." Costello, p. 117.

"Mr. Stevenson was a character . . ." Mazo and Hess, p. 60.

"Let me emphasize . . ." Nationwide TV speech 10–13–52, Shepherd and Wren, p. 56.

"Mr. Truman, Secretary Acheson . . ." *The New York Times* 10–28–52; Schnapper, p. 89.

Page 35   "He will drive . . ." Baltimore *Sun* 10–28–52; Schnapper, p. 91.

"I had hoped . . ." Bangor, Maine, 9–2–52, Shepherd and Wren, p. 53.

"You folks know . . ." Wills, p. 95.

Page 36   "Our little group . . ." *Ibid.*, p. 99.

Page 37   "General, do I have . . ." Paraphrased from Wills, p. 103: "Nixon asked Eisenhower if he meant to endorse him."

"General, do you think . . ." Nixon, p. 100.

"I know how difficult . . ." *Ibid.*

". . . there comes a time . . ." Wills, p. 104.

Page 38   "You will have to . . ." Wills, p. 105.

"My fellow Americans . . ." Checkers speech.

Page 40   "Wire and write . . ." *Ibid.*

"But I didn't . . ." Nixon, p. 117.

"I was an utter flop." Wills, p. 110.

"At least we got . . ." Nixon, p. 118.

"General, you didn't need . . ." *Ibid.*, p. 123.

"It isn't what . . ." Mazo, p. 137.

"I am opposed to pensions . . ." *Labor* 10–18–52; Shepherd and Wren, p. 110.

"If Mr. Stevenson . . ." Washington, D.C. 8–24–52, New York *Herald Tribune* 8–25–52.

"There is only one . . ." Alexandria, Va. 10–1–52, Shepherd and Wren, p. 26.

"If in order to avoid . . ." Speech before American Society of Newspaper Editors, Washington, D.C., 4–16–54, Costello, p. 121.

"It is hoped that . . ." Washington, D.C., 4–16–54, Effros, p. 16.

"Unfortunately . . ." New York *Herald-Tribune* 10–2–54; Schnapper, p. 85.

"The issue is . . ." Costello, p. 124.

"When the Eisenhower . . ." *Ibid.* p. 126.

"*Why* is the Communist Party . . ." *The New York Times* 10–24–54; Schnapper, p. 86.

"The Communist Party in America . . ." Keogh, p. 178; Schnapper, p. 88.

"Mr. Stevenson has been guilty . . ." Costello, p. 128.

"Ninety-six percent of the 6,926 Communists . . ." *Ibid.*, p. 127.

"There has come into my possession . . ." Butte, Montana, 10–22–54, Keogh, p. 177; Schnapper, p. 87.

"If there was any smearing . . ." *The New York Times* 11–2–54; Schnapper, p. 88.

"The Vietnamese lack . . ." Washington, D.C., 4–16–54, Effros, p. 172.

"There could be an honest . . ." Press Conference of Editorial Writers 10–14–57, Democratic National Committee.

Page 46   "I find it rather difficult . . ." Costello, p. 136.

"My speech will not be political." Los Angeles *News* 10–28–54; Democratic National Committee.

"I never criticize . . ." *Ibid.*

"Do you want . . ." *Ibid.*

Page 47   "I informed the President . . ." Costello, p. 147.

"The party of Schlesinger . . ." Nixon, p. 350.

"The Russian prime minister . . ." Chicago *Daily News* 10–25–56; Schnapper, p. 84.

"What Mr. Stevenson calls me . . ." Washington *Post* 10–25–54; Schnapper, p. 55.

Page 48   "But you don't win campaigns . . ." *The New York Times* 9–13–56; Schnapper, p. 39.

"It seems to me . . ." Mazo, p. 291.

Page 49   "This was not my first . . ." Nixon, p. 201.

"Take the offensive." *Ibid.*, pp. 201–02.

"You are cowards . . ." *Ibid.*, p. 202.

"I saw before me a weird-looking . . ." *Ibid.*, p. 204.

Page 50   "Not all the rioters . . ." *Ibid.*, p. 231.

"Through the courage of President Diem . . ." Chicago 10–13–58, Democratic National Committee.

"I'm sorry about that . . ." Costello, p. 293.

"As far as our candidates . . ." Oakland 10–2–58, Democratic National Committee; Schnapper, p. 67.

"This year our crop . . ." Boston *Sunday Globe* 11–16–58; Schnapper, p. 67.

Page 51   "Never before had a head of government . . ." Nixon, p. 236.

"You must not be afraid . . ." *Ibid.*, p. 254.

"There are some instances . . ." To Premier Khrushchev, Moscow, 7–24–59, Kornitzer, p. 300.

"You may be interested . . ." Nixon, p. 255.

"Later I wished I'd said . . ." American Society of Newspaper Editors, Washington, D.C., 4–18–64, Democratic National Committee.

Page 52   "It has not been . . ." *Congressional Record* 4–24–59; Schnapper, p. 124.

"Television is not so effective . . ." Mazo, p. 299.

"You know, nobody will believe it . . ." Los Angeles *Times* 3–13–60; Shepherd and Wren, p. 13.

"If you ever let . . ." White, 1961, p. 226.

Page 53   "Yes, I have spent . . ." *Ibid.*, p. 226.

"To stand here . . ." *Ibid.*

"I have no doubt whatever . . . NBC 9–11–60, Schnapper, p. 49.

"I say that just as in 1952 . . ." White, 1961, p. 226.

Page 54   "I don't believe there is . . ." Nixon, p. 328.

"The President was probably being facetious." Paraphrased from Wills, p. 124: "probably facetious."

"Inevitably, this would lead . . ." Baltimore *Sun* 5–8–60; Schnapper, p. 133.

Page 55 "For the first and only time . . ." Nixon, pp. 354–55.

"We would lose all our friends . . ." *Ibid.*, p. 355.

"Absolutely." *Saturday Evening Post* 2–25–67.

"The covert operation . . ." Nixon, p. 355.

"Jack Kennedy is going to raise . . ." White, 1961, p. 326; Schnapper, p. 152.

Page 56 "I draw the line . . ." Mazo, p. 291.

"And how is Jackie?" JFK to author, 1960.

"Matsu." From all four nationwide TV debates, 1960.

"Quemoy." *Ibid.*

"Joint TV debate . . ." Nixon, p. 357.

Page 57 "I can only say . . ." Third nationwide TV debate, 10–13–60, Wills, p. 89.

"My little daughter . . ." *The New York Times Magazine* 5–13–62.

"I brought up an issue . . ." Nixon, pp. 408–09.

Page 58 "I would find a proper legal cover . . ." de Toledano, p. 315.

"I am running for Governor . . ." *Ibid.*, p. 319.

Page 59 "California cannot afford . . ." Oakland, California, 5–4–62, Shepherd and Wren, p. 94.

"I'll dump a load . . ." *The Reporter* 8–16–62.

"It takes an awful lot . . ." Copenhagen, Denmark 7–1–62, Shepherd and Wren, p. 26.

"If elected . . ." Harris, p. 85.

"I advocate suspension . . ." *Ibid.*, p. 112.

Page 60   "What are our schools for . . ." *Ibid.*, p. 71.

"Screw them!" Witcover, p. 14.

"Now that all the members . . ." Washington *Post* 11–8–62; Schnapper, p. 136.

"Kennedy is all right . . ." Wills, p. 414.

"For sixteen years . . ." *Ibid.*, pp. 414–15.

"The press have a right . . ." Washington *Star* 11–8–62; Schnapper, p. 136.

"As I leave, I want . . ." Washington *Post* 11–8–62; Schnapper, p. 136.

Phase Two

Page 66   "An illustrious ruler . . ." Mazo, p. 251.

"I say categorically . . ." White, 1969, p. 43.

"I find when you get bored . . ." Mazo, p. 5.

Page 69   "I was in a taxicab . . ." *Saturday Evening Post* 2–25–67.

Page 70   "Red China and Russia . . ." Washington, D.C., 4–20–63, Shepherd and Wren, p. 138.

Page 71   "Looking to the future . . ." Witcover, p. 90.

"My friends in the press . . ." *Ibid.*, p. 78.

"He has struck a chord . . ." New York *Journal-American* 6–21–64; Shepherd and Wren, pp. 31–32.

Page 72   "No. It will leave . . ." Press conference, GOP convention, San Francisco 7–14–64.

"There are some . . ." Witcover, p. 98.

"Senator Goldwater . . ." Press conference, GOP convention, San Francisco 7–14–64.

"There is no substitute for victory . . ." Saigon 4–1–64, Shepherd and Wren, p. 126.

"Neutralism . . ." New York, N.Y., 4–16–64, Shepherd and Wren, p. 124.

Page 73   "The United States . . ." New York, N.Y., 3–3–64, Shepherd and Wren, p. 136.

"I am completely opposed to . . ." Schnapper, p. 128.

"I have never engaged in personalities . . ." CBS-TV interview 9–12–60, Shepherd and Wren, p. 60.

"Let's be fair . . ." New York, N.Y., 10–10–64, Shepherd and Wren, p. 52.

Page 74   "If Southeast Asia . . ." Salisbury, North Carolina, 10–10–64, Effros, p. 50.

Page 75   "The way *not* to get the Communists . . ." *Reader's Digest*, 12–65.

"Leadership requires . . ." Witcover, p. 117.

"We must never forget . . ." *The New York Times* 10–27–65; White, 1969, p. 49.

"Now that we've come . . ." Bartlesville, Oklahoma, 9–23–66, Shepherd and Wren, p. 175.

Page 76   "Now that we have hit . . ." Saigon, 8–7–66, Shepherd and Wren, p. 128.

"There is no reasonable possibility . . ." Saigon, 8–7–66, Effros, p. 163.

"The war on poverty . . ." Adler, p. 44.

"I oppose those well-intentioned . . ." ABC-TV *Issues and Answers*, 1966, Democratic National Committee.

"Just the chance of being President . . ." Louisville

Times 10–28–66; Democratic National Committee.

Page 77   "There was a big swing vote . . ." *Saturday Evening Post* 2–25–67.

"We'll kick their toes off . . ." White, 1969, p. 52.

"I have great concern . . ." New York, N.Y., 12–31–67, Shepherd and Wren, p. 171.

"I believe the Republican nominee . . ." Washington, D.C., 10–18–67, Shepherd and Wren, p. 176.

Page 78   "We had a very interesting discussion . . ." de Toledano, p. 333.

"No politician is dead . . ." *National Observer* 10–16–67; Schnapper, p. 23.

"They still call me Tricky Dick." *National Review* 11–67; Schnapper, p. 18.

"We simply cannot afford to . . ." *Foreign Affairs* 10–67; Shepherd and Wren, p. 139.

"In my job you can't enjoy . . ." Alsop, p. 195; Schnapper, p. 16.

Page 79   "This is a generation . . ." *Saturday Evening Post*, 2–25–67.

"The decision to go to war . . ." Portland *Oregonian* 4–22–67; Schnapper, p. 114.

"I will not shift my position . . ." Los Angeles *Times* 10–19–67; Schnapper, p. 114.

"If you're asking me . . ." *National Review* 11–14–67.

"I'm not going to take . . ." Washington *Star* 11–23–67.

"Some people say I oversimplify." *Saturday Evening Post*, 2–25–67.

"The establishment press . . ." *Saturday Evening Post* 12–2–67.

"Okay, I blew up in 1962." *National Review* 11–14–67; Schnapper, p. 137.

Page 80   "Ladies and gentlemen . . ." Adler, p. 17.

"Never in the history . . ." *Newsweek* 5–20–68; Shepherd and Wren, p. 119.

"This country cannot tolerate . . ." *Time* 3–1–68; Shepherd and Wren, p. 131.

"I'm not going to sit here . . ." *The Progressive* 3–68; Schnapper, p. 45.

Page 81   "I wouldn't charge Lyndon . . ." New York *Post* 3–9–68; Schnapper, p. 45.

Page 82   "This country must move . . ." White, 1969, p. 131.

"I eat cottage cheese . . ." Washington *Star* 5–27–68; Schnapper, p. 38.

"I believe in hitting back . . ." Alsop, p. 124; Schnapper, p. 40.

"Sock it to me!" NBC-TV, *Laugh-In*, 1968.

"The three passions . . ." Schnapper, p. 23.

"While all this . . ." *Ibid.*

"Voters quickly forget . . ." Nixon, p. 330.

Page 83   "In times of trouble . . ." *Look* 3–5–68; Schnapper, p. 71.

"I have serious doubts . . ." CBS 5–24–68, Schnapper, p. 122.

"For most of us . . ." Acceptance speech, GOP convention, Miami Beach 8–8–68, *U.S. News & World Report* 8–19–68.

"I think it possible . . ." Washington *Post* 4–20–68; Schnapper, p. 115.

"I've always thought . . ." White, 1969, p. 147.

Page 86   "The Johnson Administration . . ." *The New York Times* 10–2–68.

Page 87   "Conditions are different . . ." *U.S. News & World Report* 8–19–68.

"This time we're going to win!" Acceptance speech, GOP convention, Miami Beach 8–8–68, *U.S. News & World Report* 8–19–68.

Page 88   "A man of compassion." McGinniss, p. 68.

"There can be a mystique . . ." Wills, p. 285.

"If you want your President . . ." *Time* 11–1–68.

Page 89   "I and Agnew will question . . ." Witcover, p. 392.

"I picked Spiro Agnew . . ." *New York* magazine 10–28–68.

"In a Nixon administration . . ." 9–9–68, Democratic National Committee.

"The real answer to progress . . ." *New York* magazine 10–28–68.

Page 90   "No, no, I have no plans . . ." *Ibid.*

Page 91   "We're going to build this . . ." *McGinniss*, p. 79.

"I sweat too much." *Ibid.*, p. 14.

"I say that after four years . . ." White, 1969, p. 387.

"No one with this responsibility . . ." New York, N.Y., 3–10–68, Effros, p. 219.

Page 92   "Do you like the work?" *Newsweek* 1–25–71; Evans and Novak, p. 7.

"In Deshler, Ohio . . ." White, 1969, p. 396.

"If I had my life to live over . . ." *Newsweek* 12–22–69.

Page 93 "America has suffered from . . ." Inaugural Address 1–20–69.

"An era of confrontation . . ." *Ibid.*

Page 97 "In the sense that . . ." *The New York Times* 2–28–69.

"Cease-fire is a term of art . . ." *The New York Times* 1–28–69.

"The policy of this country . . ." *Ibid.*

Page 98 "My advisers tell me . . ." *Ibid.*

"I do not see a reasonable . . ." The Nixon-Agnew Campaign Committee, p. 119.

"I do not go along . . ." *The New York Times* 1–28–69.

"There is no prospect . . ." *The New York Times* 3–15–69; Effros, p. 200.

"It is a safeguard . . ." *The New York Times* 3–15–69.

Page 99 "We have no plans . . ." *The New York Times* 4–19–69.

"I will make this promise . . ." *Time* 5–2–69.

"I have decided to order . . ." Midway Island, 6–8–69, Effros, p. 200.

"I should just like to give you . . ." Address at Air Force Academy, Colorado Springs, 6–4–69.

Page 100 "The American war dead . . ." *Ibid.*

Page 101 "We cannot learn from one another . . ." Inaugural Address 1–20–69.

"As far as how many . . ." *The New York Times* 6–20–69.

The source for Nixon's conversations with soldiers, beginning with "And where are you from?" and ending with "Do they ever get any . . ." is *Newsweek,* 8–11–69.

Page 102 "I think that history will . . ." Saigon, 7–30–69, Effros, p. 152.

"Under no circumstances will I . . ." Quoted in White House press release 10–13–69, "Exchange of letters between President and Randy J. Dicks."

Page 103 "Fifteen Years ago . . ." Nationwide TV and radio speech, 11–3–69.

Page 105 "We stand firm . . ." *New Republic* 10–17–70.

Page 108 "What appears was certainly a massacre . . ." *The New York Times* 12–9–69.

"I have examined the charges . . ." Washington *Post* 10–21–69.

"In fact, my acquaintance . . ." *Ibid.*

". . . the one person entrusted . . ." *The New York Times* 10–22–71.

Page 109 ". . . that the day will come . . ." *Time* 4–20–70.

"As long as the Senate . . ." Statement by President, White House press release 4–9–70.

"Yes. I would. I'm not . . ." *U.S. News & World Report* 2–9–70.

Page 110 "We must balance our Federal . . ." State of the Union message 1–22–70.

"We had a balanced budget . . ." *Ibid.*

"In spite of the fact . . ." *Ibid.*

"So long as I am in the White House . . ." From the President's statement on the National Commission on Obscenity and Pornography, 10–24–70.

Page 111 "I am against the proposals . . ." *U.S. News & World Report* 3–29–71.

"There are no American ground combat troops . . ." *U.S. News & World Report* 3–16–70.

Page 112 "These developments in Cambodia . . ." Press conference in President's office, White House press release, 3–21–70.

"Well, as a California voter . . ." *Ibid.*

"I am confident . . ." *Ibid.*

"The rate of unemployment . . ." *Ibid.*

Page 113 "One, this country is not in a recession . . ." *Ibid.*

"In achieving desegregation we . . ." *U.S. News & World Report* 4–6–70.

"Only to the extent that . . ." *New Republic* 12–26–70.

Page 114 "Tonight American and South Vietnamese units . . ." Nationwide TV and radio address 4–30–70.

"A majority of the American people . . ." *Ibid.*

Page 115 "If when the chips are down . . ." *Ibid.*

"Others are saying . . ." *Ibid.*

"Whether I may be a one-term President . . ." *Ibid.*

Page 116 "We expect the Soviets . . ." As quoted by Senator Albert Gore in *The New York Times* 5–6–70; Effros, p. 157.

(154)

"This should remind us . . ." Statement 5–4–70, Democratic National Committee.

"You know, you see these bums . . ." Informal conference at Defense Department 5–1–70, Democratic National Committee.

"I would certainly regret . . ." Press conference 5–8–70, Democratic National Committee.

"No, I have not been surprised . . ." *Ibid.*

"Why, I really love . . ." Osborne, p. 75.

"I told them how in 1939 . . ." *The New York Times* 5–10–70; *Time* 5–18–70.

The sources for the muddled meeting at the Memorial beginning with "I know you think we are a bunch of sons of bitches" and ending with "He just kept saying 'have a really nice day'" are: *The New York Times* 5–10–70; *Time* 5–18–70; *Hard Times* June 15–22, 1970.

"I can now state . . ." Nationwide TV and radio address on the Cambodian Sanctuary Operation 6–3–70.

". . . somebody that was nothing . . ." Osborne, p. 129.

"Instead of just sitting . . ." *Ibid.*

"Young people glorify wrongdoers . . ." *Newsweek* 8–17–70.

"I noted for example . . ." *Ibid.*

"It usually goes a couple of minutes . . ." *Ibid.*

"I said charged." *Time* 8–17–70.

"As you know . . ." Nationwide TV and radio address on the New Initiative for Peace in Southeast Asia 10–7–70.

Page 123   "Let me say . . ." Osborne, p. 164.

"The time has come . . ." *Time* 11–16–70.

Page 124   "That's what they hate to see!" *Time* 11–9–70.

"There is no cause that justifies . . ." *The New York Times* 10–30–70.

"The election . . ." *Time* 11–16–70.

Page 125   "I think that's a legitimate criticism." *Newsweek* 12–21–70.

"Any lady who is First Lady . . ." *U.S. News & World Report* 3–22–71.

Page 126   "A revolution as profound . . ." State of the Union message 1–22–71.

"The tide of inflation . . ." *Ibid.*

"Inflation will be further reduced . . ." *Ibid.*

"We should take no comfort . . ." *Ibid.*

"It will be a full-employment budget . . ." *Ibid.*

Page 127   "I do not plan to ask for . . ." Nationwide TV and radio conversation with four correspondents 12–4–71.

"I am now a Keynesian . . ." Evans and Novak, p. 372.

"I think there is no substitute . . ." Nationwide TV and radio conversation with Howard K. Smith, ABC, 3–22–71.

Page 128   "Before any final sentence . . ." *New Republic* 4–17–71.

"Not strictly legal . . ." *Ibid.*

"This is sort of in the heart . . ." *Ibid.*

"I have never called . . ." Drury, p. 395.

"I am not an expert . . ." *U.S. News & World Report* 3–29–71.

"As for the family . . ." *Ibid.*

Page 129 "To look at America . . ." Bicentennial TV and radio broadcast from the National Archives 7–3–71.

Page 130 "The time has come . . ." *Ibid.*

"I shall go to China." Nationwide TV broadcast 7–15–71.

"I am today ordering a freeze . . ." Nationwide TV and radio address 8–15–71.

"Fuck the ABA." *New Republic,* 11–6–71.

About the Author

Gore Vidal was born at West Point. In 1943
he graduated from the Phillips Exeter Academy and
enlisted in the army. While in the Pacific, at the age
of nineteen, he wrote the much-praised novel
Williwaw. Among his other novels are *The City
and The Pillar, Julian, Washington, D.C.,
Myra Breckinridge* and *Two Sisters.*